From Ghosties and Ghoulies and long
leggittie beasties and things that go
bump in the night

GOOD LORD DELIVER US!

Al Durrance

Printed by
Durra Print, Inc.
717 South Woodward Ave.
Tallahassee, Florida 32304
(850) 222-4768

Foreword

IF THE TITLE OF THIS BOOK attracted you, the contents will more than satisfy your desire to know more about this seldom written or spoken about subject.

I have known Al and Julia Durrance and their four boys for more than fifteen years, and have held prayer-workshops in churches Al has pastored. His two-hour long treatment of the Holy Spirit in both Old and New Testament gave me a whole new and fresh understanding of God's will for us in giving individuals the Holy Spirit for the upbuilding of His church.

The gifts given to Al Durrance have been the basis for his teaching and his counselling. The people who have been set free and delivered from various kinds of ''ghoulies and ghosties'' are grateful to God for the deliverance ministry God has given to him. A dear friend of mine was one of these, and the freedom she now enjoys has opened a wide door of spiritual ministry for her in her own church.

This book is long over-due, and may God put it into the hands of those who need it and can use it.

—Rosalind Rinker

About the Author

AL DURRANCE has been active in the ministry of the Episcopal Church for over thirty years. A native Floridian he served parishes there and moved to eastern N. C. in 1981. Since retiring from active parish work, he has become the North American Warden of the International Order of St. Luke the Physician. He is a speaking leader at CFO's and conducts retreats and conferences inside and outside of the Episcopal Church. He sees Christian healing as a normal manifestation of the presence of the Kingdom of God.

Introduction

ONE OF THE GREAT PHILOSOPHICAL problems of man through the ages has been the understanding of good and evil. He has handled the problem in many different ways; but the Christian has usually considered the struggle as one between God and Satan.

I had always assumed the same conflict until I was working on my thesis for my master's degree. When I went back to review the writing in the Old Testament, I found that there was no conflict between God and Satan. God was the author of both good and evil. Satan was simply a tool.

That is not a very popular Christian viewpoint, but it is never the less the Old Testament view. The New Testament yields an entirely different story. There is not simply a cleaning up of the Old Creation; there is an entirely new creation in Christ Jesus.

In this New Creation there is no place for Satan. The Torah is no longer seen as a demand, but as a fulfilled promise. The basis of life changes from law to love. There is no evil and as a result no conflict between good and evil.

It appeared to me that the conflict between good and evil was not between God and Satan. That battle has been decided, and Satan is at best a tool that God allows to be judge, jury and executioner under the Law. He has no power but that allowed him.

The conflict is between the Old and the New Creations. We are born into the Old, we have been called by Jesus into the New. The decision to remain in the Old Creation under the dominion of Satan, or enter the New Creation under the dominion of Jesus is a choice we all must make.

Once the decision is made, we are set free from the power of Satan by passing through death into life. The greater power of God's love in Jesus Christ was able to set us free—not simply when we come to the end of life in this body, but while we are yet in the body of flesh and blood.

The early Christian Church used exorcism in the power of the Name of Jesus to prove the superiority of the Christian faith over the religions of that day. The early writers tell us that the exorcist in the Name of Jesus is able to make even the gods of the temples come out of those who desire to be set free.

My good friend, Frank Costantino who has been very active in prison ministry asked that I write a book about exorcism that was not grounded in fear of the devil. I wrote this book in 1980 for that purpose. Finding no publisher at that time, I relegated it to the shelf until recent months.

Those who have read the manuscript over the years have found it helpful in understanding their own struggles with good and evil, and some have urged me to have it printed. It is for this reason that I have put it into print hoping that it might be of help to others who are seeking some new way to view God's revelation of old truth.

I make no claim to exclusive truth. Only God can make that claim. What I have written is based on the Scriptural texts of the Old and New Testaments. I simply wish to share one view of God and His two covenant relationships with mankind that has been helpful to me, and I hope may be to you.

Table of Contents

Deliverance 1

A Historical Perspective 13

The Origin and Nature of Man 22

The Problem of Evil 33

The Example of Jesus 48

Deliverance and Authority 57

Sanctification—Being Set Free 70

The Occult—Confusion, Fascination and Bondage 77

Spiritualism 87

Reincarnation—The Ultimate in Recycling 95

Symptoms and Solutions 101

Ghosts, Gates and Gospel 113

Delivered into Life 117

Deliverance

IN SOME CIRCLES of the Christian community, deliverance has become just another word for exorcism. In reality the whole of the Christian Gospel is directed toward deliverance. We are to be delivered from Sin into righteousness. We are to be delivered from the old creation, which is passing away, into the new creation in Christ Jesus which is eternal.

Until we see the whole picture, it is hard to make sense out of any of the parts. One of the old Welch litanies prays to God for a number of things. Among them is a quaint petition which goes, "From ghosties and ghoulies and long leggitie beasties and things that go bump in the night, GOOD LORD, DELIVER US." It then goes on to ask for deliverance from our own human nature that keeps us from God—from blindness of heart; from pride, vainglory and hypocrisy; from envy, hatred and malice; and from a multitude of other things. They knew that we needed deliverance; and they were of a mind to ask God for it.

God is not content for us simply to be delivered from the negative things of our lives, He is concerned that we be delivered into the positive aspects of the new life—the life in His eternal Kingdom. The Kingdom of God is not somewhere above the sky as many people think. Space does not separate us from the Kingdom of God. It is not far ahead in the future. Time does not separate us from the Kingdom of God. The Kingdom of God is at hand. It is here—close enough to see and enter. It is the presence of the risen Christ reigning in the lives of the people of God. This is the goal toward which we are called—the Kingdom into which we are to be delivered.

There are a multitude of tools that God has given us to use for deliverance. With each tool He gives us the authority to wield it. He has given His Church the authority to forgive Sin. That means more than excusing everything that we have done. It means that we have been given the power to break through to the heart of man's life to set him free from the things that move him to act sinfully. Confession is one of the most neglected ministries of the Church; and yet it embodies the one authority that Jesus has imparted to the Church when He breathed on them and said, "Receive ye the Holy Ghost. Whose soever sins ye remit, they are remitted unto them; and whose soever sins ye retain, they are retained." Jn 20:22-23.

We so often preach this forgiveness in the power of the cross, and then proceed to condemn those of our brethren who do not agree with us. In order for us to deliver others from Sin, and be delivered ourselves, we must be aware of the forgiveness that God has given us. We must know the power of love that cannot be contained in self righteousness. It must be exercised in setting men free from the burden of guilt and anxiety that plagues Americans today.

I was sitting in on a seminar on spirituality one day, and the leader was making a point of how little we think of ourselves. He said, "If you were God, you would very likely let everyone go to heaven except yourself." The statement was a bit shocking; but the thing that struck me was the nodding heads of the people as they gave assent to what he had said. It was a demonstration of our failure to really accept the authority of God so that we might give and receive His forgiveness and be set free.

Most of the people in the room were "born again" believers. They were not adulterers or murderers. Some may have been a little less than honest on income tax; but none of them were thieves in the common sense of the word. They were people who had been abused by others. They had been subjected to authorities who had used fear and guilt to make them conform to some desired behavior pattern. They had been manipulated into a conformity that made freedom difficult for them to attain.

In her effort to bring men to righteousness, the Church has often neglected the promise of God, and tried to employ fear and guilt by threatening men with hell. She brings into bondage the very people God has sent her to set free. We might add to the old litany, "From fear of rejection and condemnation, from man's judgment, and from all negative proclamations, Good Lord, deliver us." The proclamation of the gospel is clear, and has been from the beginning, "Jesus Christ died that we might be forgiven all of our Sins."

The Church has been entrusted with the revelation of God in Jesus Christ. She has been given the authority to set men free from ignorance. There are many who have no experience of the Kingdom of God because they do not know that there is a Kingdom. Their deliverance rests in our willingness to share what we have received from Jesus Christ. To be sure, we hold these treasures in earthen vessels; but we do hold them. They have been poured out for us that we might be reconciled, and that we might receive the ministry of reconciliation. We are to know God and make Him known to all men.

Revelation is not simply that body of doctrine that has been passed on to us from those who have gone before us in our tradition. Revelation is both knowledge about and knowing of God that grows out of living in a personal relationship with the King Himself. Revelation is more than knowing about; it must include our entering into a personal relationship wherein we know Him. It is on the basis of this knowing relationship that we can talk intelligibly about God to others who know Him. If I have not met Him, if I have not had some communication with Him; then I am hard pressed to share Him with others. I cannot introduce you to someone I do not know myself.

Martin Buber, the great Jewish mystic referred to this kind of relationship as an "I-Thou" relationship. It is a knowing of God in the conversational sense as one to whom you speak and listen. He is more than the one you talk or hear about. Most of us have had some experience of an "Aha!" It is a sudden dawning on us that we know some reality. It is an awareness that all we have heard is actually true—that God can be known and in some way we know Him.

These moments cannot be sustained in the average Christian life; but as we grow, we can seek them with increasing frequency. We can consciously seek out that encounter to which we have been called by God in prayer with regularity. We can also sustain the duration by receiving the gift of awareness of His presence. We can never hold that awareness with striving, but with resting in His presence.

God has not hidden from man. It was man who hid from God in the Garden of Eden. It is man who has been hiding ever since. Jesus is the light that comes into the world to enlighten every man. Those who are evil do not come to the light because they do not want their deeds to be known. As we receive Jesus in our own lives, we become the light of the world. If the world is going to be delivered from its darkness, it will be by a Church which has received the revelation of God in Christ, and is willing to share that revelation with others.

Healing is a ministry of the Church that has come to some measure of restoration in the past century. For a time it was lost in both superstition and rationalism. It has come back to us through two major channels in the Church. The sacramental and liturgical churches have carried a ministry of healing through the ages. It has not always been strong, but there have been a number of quiet miracles that have occurred through the years. They have been found both at altars where men have prayed for healing, and at shrines that God has set apart to show forth His healing power and love.

The second tradition has come through the pentecostal wing of the Church. In their zeal for the Spirit of God, the pentecostal people have dared to read the scriptures as if they are literally true. They did not know, as some believe, that God had withdrawn the power of the Spirit from the Church at the close of the Apostolic Age. They offered themselves as channels for the healing power of God; and God manifested His healing through them.

They were very much like the bumble bee. Every aeronautical engineer knows that the bumble bee cannot fly. His body is too heavy to be supported by the size of his wings. With this weight to wing ratio, it is impossible for the bumble bee to fly at all. Fortunately, the bumble bee does not know that, and so he flies anyway.

Over the years, the evidence for spiritual healing has become so weighty that even the medical profession has come to acknowledge it in some measure. There are even some Christian medical groups that have been established to promote the use of spiritual healing together with the healing gifts of the medical profession. Doctor William S. Reed, in Tampa, Florida has established the Christian Medical Foundation, and he has coined the term logo-psycho-somatic which means that man is more than a soul and body. He is a spirit soul and body; and he must be treated as such if we are to treat him as a whole man.

For the Bible Christian or the traditional Christian, healing is a normal part of our heritage. We are instructed to call both our doctor and our clergyman as we encounter illness. We support the healing process with prayer throughout. We are delivered from sickness to health by the power of God's presence in our lives.

Exorcism, or casting out demons, has always been a source of fear for many. For others it has been a source of freedom. Some do not like to believe that there are demons in the world in which we live; but what we want to believe is not always the truth. I recall a conversation that I had with a seminary professor about the issue of the demonic and the power of God to deal with it. At the end of our conversation, he said, ''I do not want to live in a world that is filled with devils; and so I do not believe that.''

His way of dealing with reality is not rare. People generally believe what they want to believe. There are some things that are costly or painful to believe, but we feel that not believing would be worse, so we hold on to our belief. My seminary professor finds it painful to live in a world where devils abound. He feels that it is easier for him to live in the chaos of the world as if it is a natural thing than it would be for him to have to deal with the demonic.

When I was working on a seminary paper on exorcism, I read all of the material I could find on the subject. Among the reading was some material written from a psychological viewpoint. The authors tended to reject any possibility of the reality of demons. They had not encountered any situation they could not explain psychologically. They did not want to believe in demons, and they made no effort to verify their existence through experimental means.

On one hand they claimed scientific status; on the other hand they avoided scientific method.

Scientific method is no mysterious thing. It simply means that we try something before we talk about it with authority. One of the experiments we used to do in physical chemistry lab was to check the freezing point of water. It was a simple experiment in which we put a thermometer in pure water and cooled it down until it began to freeze. It always turned out to be 32 °F. That is an experience that gives us information. It is called scientific method.

If we are to speak of the demonic in terms of scientific data and conclusions, we have to be willing to try it out and see. I once asked a friend of mine who was in a counselling center to go along with a testing program to confirm the benefits of exorcism and the reality of the demonic. His reply was that it would be too difficult to set up a well controlled experiment. I then had an idea that we might set up a testing program to disprove the effectiveness of exorcism as being a reality; and he said that we really didn't want to do that. The fact was that he did not want to try it out to see what would happen.

When I first became aware of the reality of demons and the use of exorcism in dealing with them, I found myself involved in the experience before I knew what I was about. I found that I was dealing with something in people that seemed like forces other than the people themselves. It seemed like the cases of demon possession that I had read about in scripture. I thought that I had better find out what my resources were in dealing with them.

The Church offered me little more than an uneasiness. The scriptures were and are aware of the problem. In the gospels we are charged by Jesus to set men free. We are to use all of the authority and knowledge we can lay hold of—not simply that which is comfortable. It became apparent that some people find release through the ministration of exorcism. That makes it a valuable tool for our use in the Body of Christ.

When people in the parish began to experience the power of Jesus through exorcism, we felt that we had the key to clean up the Church if not the world. We tried using exorcism on every problem that arose. We did not solve them all, but we did learn some things. We learned that all problems are not caused by demons; but some are. That was a conclusion that we reached by scientific method.

We also learned that we could cast out demons forever without any lasting effect unless people were willing and ready to grow in the Spirit. Deliverance is more than removing demons; it is growing fruit unto righteousness. It seems to be very much like gardening. When I plant a garden, I pull only the weeds that are blocking the growth of the fruit. Those are the only ones that have to be pulled.

I remember once pulling all of the weeds out of a garden so it would be clear for growing vegetables. When the ground cover was removed, it was difficult to get anything to start back because the ground cover was gone, and nothing held moisture. I had a friend who was cleaned out completely through the use of exorcism, and he went through great anxiety because he felt that he was not a real person. What he had known to be his inner self had been removed without the infilling with some better alternative. He is whole today, but growth into the new person was difficult. It is far better to weed out only that which blocks our growth.

We have been given the authority of Christ to exercise this ministry to set the people of God free—not as some magical incantation, but in the power of the Name of Jesus to whom every knee must bow. If we are to deliver people from bondage into the freedom of the Kingdom of God, this tool must be a part of our kit to minister to those who are sore pressed by spiritual enemies.

Hugh W. White, father of Agnes Sanford, was a missionary to China for years. After his experience with that culture, he wrote a book called *Demonism: Verified and Analyzed.* His concern was to show the reality of possession in lands where other religions held sway. He was also convinced that the reason there is little possession in the United States is because we have been basically a Christian land. With the deterioration of the morality and the increasing practice of other religions in this country, we will see an increase of demonic activity in the country. The Church is called to be prepared to meet this crisis as it arises.

There is no need for a Christian to fear; but we cannot afford to be complacent. We have been given the power and authority to deal with the demonic in life as it arises—not in our own strength, but in the grace and power of God's creative love. We must realize, however, that we cannot use something we do not know. It is good for us to have some idea of the scope of bondage from which we must be set free—and kept free.

The basic foundation of our freedom is Jesus Christ. We must be born again in Him. That is a term that has been so widely used that it has a variety of meanings. We usually tie it to our own experience, and then we seek to tie our experience to everyone else. We often become like the lady who fell in the well in her back yard. While she was there waiting to be rescued, she met the Lord and gave her life to Him. When she was rescued, her experience meant so much to her that she spent the rest of her life pushing people down her well.

The Gospel of John uses the term in the third chapter in a manner that might help us unlock the meaning. It is not a matter of some particular emotional experience. It is a matter of the resulting condition in our lives. ''Except you be born again by water and the Holy Spirit, you cannot enter into the Kingdom of God." Jn 3:5 The key to knowing that we are born again lies in our awareness of the Kingdom of God in our life right now. If I have been born again, the evidence will be my capacity to see and enter into that relationship with God wherein I know Him as my Lord and King. He reigns as King in my life now, in the midst of His creation.

It matters not what my experience has been. It might have been electric or it might have been the most peaceful of encounters with the risen Christ. It is the established relationship that becomes the key. By the same token, if I am unaware of the presence of God in His creation where I am; then I have not become aware of my new birth (whether I have been born again or not). No measure of emotional experience can be called a "born again" experience until I can see and enter the Kingdom. Once we realize that truth, we are more open to get our eyes off our experience and onto the Kingdom in which we are called to walk.

As we are born again, two things happen to us. We begin to die with Christ; and we begin to be raised up with Christ. There is no way out of this world that is not tied to our death and resurrection in Jesus. Our true deliverance consists in cooperating with God as He brings us through death in the old creation into life in the new.

When we are born again, we are babes in Christ. We are not mature from the moment of our birth. Paul points out to the people of Corinth that their divisions are evidence that they are babes in Christ—they are carnal men. That part of us that is still carnal is still subject to the powers of this world. It is open to being obsessed and buffeted by the prince of darkness. The whole of the old creation has been given to him. It has been subjected to vanity in hope. Its hope is to see, to know, and to choose Jesus Christ as Savior and Lord. He is our one ticket out of the old into the new. He is our one Way in Whom we might grasp and know the love of God that He has given us. He is the one Way we can be delivered from the old into the new—into God's eternal Kingdom.

Deliverance must be more than eliminating negative forces in my life. If I were to stop doing all of the bad things that were forbidden when I was a child, I would still not be delivered. I might no longer act sinfully, but I would not really be alive either. The Christian faith is not based on the "Thou shalt nots" of the Bible. It hangs on the "Thou shalts." If I cease from my sinning without finding and working at my vocation from God, I shall be living in righteousness in one sense; but I shall also be living in death.

One of the basic assumptions that I was taught when I was a child was that all men were basically good. They simply need to be educated. They need to be taught the right things so that they might live together in peace and harmony. The idea is absurd. History has shown us repeatedly that men are born striving to build a kingdom of self. They fight their way through life until they come into contact with the Kingdom of God, or they find their way into the loneliness that the kingdom of self must bring.

Original Sin does not speak of original guilt. It is the very basic statement that no man, as he is born into the world, is pure in heart. That remains for God to work out in our lives as we become open to His grace. We were born of the flesh, and we must be born of the Spirit if we are to be set free. Our original Sin is that sin which we find at the origin of the human race as we know it today. We see ourselves as God. We grasp the power and the authority, where we can, to impose on others our own ideas of good and evil. Until our transformation by the grace of God, we remain unable to do anything that is good. We remain in bondage to the self, the world and the devil.

Our deliverance is described by St. Paul as our adoption as the children of God. "For you have not received the spirit of bondage to fear, but you have received the spirit of adoption whereby we cry 'Abba! Father!' The Spirit bears witness with our spirit that we are the children of God." Rm 8:15-16 The Holy Spirit works within us to recreate us as new creatures.

This adoption is the beginning of our positive walk with God. It is the beginning of our coming to know God as our personal and loving Father. The Trinity of God is a mystery. That does not mean that God cannot be known. It means that He cannot be understood. We cannot ever understand God. That would require that we have the same experience that He has. If we could understand God, He would be less than we are. We can KNOW God. That is an altogether different thing.

I have lived with my wife over twenty-five years. I still do not understand her, but I know her. I find God much the same. I have known God for over twenty-five years, but I still do not understand Him. It is in knowing God that I have come to know the Trinity of God. I have also come to understand that it is something to be experienced. It is NOT something to be understood and explained.

I am called to know God as my Father. I am called to see that it is He who has given me direction and purpose in life—both this one and the next. I have come to see that He has revealed that purpose to me in Jesus Christ. I know Jesus as my Savior. It is He who lifted me out of my old life and set me in His new one. It is Jesus who has broken then the bonds that have bound me (not all of them quite yet) so that I can know in part the glorious liberty of the children of God.

I know Him from time to time as Lord. It is my deepest desire to know

Him all of the time as Lord. I long for the day when I no longer take the bit in my teeth and try to get God to ''do it my way.'' I know the Holy Spirit when I say yes to God in me. It is He who brings the strength of God into my weakness. He is the one who breathes life into my dying. The Holy Spirit is not as some would like to say, unpredictable. He is as predictable as the sun coming up in the morning. Where ever the Holy Spirit works, He works to incarnate Jesus Christ within us and through us for others.

To know God as Trinity is to know Him as Father, Son and Holy Spirit. It is to see that the teaching of Jesus that John records is true. ''When the Spirit of truth comes, he will guide you into all truth; for he will not speak on his own authority, but whatever he hears he will speak, and he will declare to you the things that are to come. He will glorify me, for he will take what is mine and declare it to you. All that the Father has is mine, therefore I said that he will take what is mine and declare it to you.'' Jn 16:13-15

My deliverance means that I must relinquish my self-sufficiency. There is no more room in the Kingdom of God for self-sufficiency than there is for self righteousness. We are all totally dependent upon God to begin with; and we are interdependent one with another. I cannot live as a Christian without the rest of the Body of Christ. I cannot find my perfection without seeking yours. We are so constructed that God has arranged us in an organic union with Himself and with one another.

Jesus said it very simply. ''For whoever would save his life will lose it; and whoever loses his life for my sake and the gospel's will save it.'' Mk 8:35 When I die to self, I do not cease to exist; I come into a new existence. I come into a reality that is superior to all other realities. I come not by my own works but by His. It is God who works within me to will and to do His own good pleasure.

We are all called in the light of Jesus to seek our new birth and the new power to fulfill our vocation. This is our deliverance as we live as children of God growing from babes into mature ones. We are no longer to wander through the world trying to make the world conform to our image for it. We are not to try to remove ourselves from the world. We are to become one with Jesus Christ in the power of the Holy Spirit. We are called to know who we are as the children of God and heirs of the Kingdom.

God seeks to bring us to emotional wholeness. We are not called to live in bondage to fear. The fear of the Lord may be the beginning of wisdom; but the end of wisdom is love. John tells us there is no fear in love, for perfect love casts out fear. We are to live without anxiety and worry. Jesus pointed out that no one can add one cubit to the measure of his stature by being anxious. We are to seek first God's Kingdom and His righteousness. The rest will be added.

St. Paul admonishes us to deal with anger rather than let it bring us to sin. We are not to let the sun go down on our wrath. There are some who seek to justify their anger; but I do not find that is helpful to them. Whether we call it anger or righteous indignation, it still takes its toll within us. We get angry or hurt when our expectations are not met, and as James says, "The wrath of man worketh not the righteousness of God." Ja 1:20

Emotional wholeness means that we are to trade in all of the fleshly reactions that keep us in bondage, and allow the Holy Spirit to grow in us His fruit—that we might reflect in our lives the character that Jesus revealed in His. The fruit of the Spirit—all of the many forms of love—constitute emotional wholeness that the world cannot give or take away. It is the gift that God wills for all of us to receive as we prepare for a more complete life with Him. In the Kingdom, there is only one love, for God Himself is love.

We are intended to have mental wholeness. We are called to know who we are. We are to be informed about how to live in the world. We are not to get our education from the world but from the Lord. It is Jesus' will that we be IN the world, but not OF the world. The prepositions are clear—IN but not OF.

We live where we are, but we receive our initiative from God. God has commanded us to love Him with all of our heart, all of our soul, and all of our MIND. We are rational beings, and God did not add the reason just to entertain us. It is His will that we have the mind of Christ that He might think with our hearts and our minds. They are given for His use in us as we present Him to the world.

I was in a seminar one day listening to a lecture and trying to stay awake, when the speaker said, "God gave us a mind so we could use it."

I had heard that statement many times before. I had even said it myself, but this time it caught my attention. It did not witness to my spirit, and so I turned to the Lord and asked, "Lord, did you give us a mind so that we could use it?"

I was surprised to hear, "No!"

I couldn't let the issue drop there, I was fascinated by the possibility of the mind having another use. "What did you give it to us for?"

His answer was very simple, "So that I could use it."

I have never been one to do things unnecessarily, and it occurred to me that under the circumstances, I might leave the rest of the lecture and go take a nap. If the Lord was going to use my mind, I thought He ought to know enough for both of us. I had to ask before I left, "Lord, why do I have to learn this stuff then?"

God's humor was in the answer, "Have you ever tried to cut down a tree with a dull axe? Your mind must be sharp for me to use.''

We are to have physical wholeness. We are to invite God to work in every fiber of our being with the creative power of His love that is able to set us free to be healthy. Any good physician will acknowledge that he can treat a patient, but he cannot heal him. God is the only one who can heal. It is God that has built into the creation a drive to strive for wholeness. At times it is the doctor rather than the theologian that has grasped this fact. The doctor knows that he can help in the process. He can remove certain barriers to healing; but he cannot generate the new tissue that is necessary to the healing process.

Prayer seems to open the way for healing. Prayer is not the effort to make God change His mind about a person and heal them. It is the effort on our part to open the windows of life for God to reach through and do His will on earth as in heaven. Estelle Carver, a great saint of God, used to say that prayer was simply putting someone together with God. It is an action that is both positive and passive. It is positive in that it intends to open the way for God. It is passive in that it intends to allow God to work His will, and even conform our will to His.

I heard someone on TV once say, ''Prayer moves the hand of God.'' Nothing could be farther from the truth. That would mean that we can move the hand of God. The truth is that God moves the hand of God. Prayer is our invitation for Him to come in and accomplish His will in us. God's will is that we be made whole, but He will not impose His will. Our prayer does not command God to move; it offers Him the opportunity to make our wholeness a reality.

There is only one way that we might learn to walk in the Kingdom that God has prepared for us. We learn to walk in the Kingdom as we learned to walk in the flesh. We learn to walk by walking. There is no book that we can read. There is no teacher—other than Jesus—to whom we can listen that will enable us to walk in the Kingdom of God. Our learning process lies in our willingness to step out in faith and try God.

Paul admonishes the Romans, ''I beseech you brethren, by the mercies of God that you offer your bodies a living sacrifice, which is your reasonable service. And be not conformed to this world, but be ye transformed by the renewing of your mind, proving what is that good and acceptable and perfect will of God.'' Rm 12:1 It happens when we are willing to challenge God—to test His faithfulness by committing Him to action. Until we commit God to action in our lives, we can never know for sure that His promises are true.

The early Christian church knew this by experience. They did not have a brief single encounter with God, and then begin to live the Christian life under their own steam. They walked daily in his presence. They trusted Him to lead them daily. They met Him in the preaching, they experienced Him in the continued healing of mind, body and spirit that they all knew beyond the first encounter. They knew Him to be present. They knew Him to be ministering through the people whom He had called to be His own. As they experienced His presence in their daily lives, they realized what it meant to walk in the Kingdom of God.

A Historical Perspective

DELIVERANCE IS MUCH MORE than casting out demons. It is a complete change from the old creation which is passing away because it has been made subject to corruption. It is an introduction to the new life in God's Kingdom. We might even see it as being cast out of the old creation into the new. It is a process of being set free from all bondage to walk in the glorious liberty of the children of God.

Jesus sent His disciples to preach the gospel, to heal the sick and to cast out demons. "So they went out and preached that men should repent. And they cast out many demons, and anointed many with oil who were sick and healed them." Mk 6:12-13   They saw the commission to go forth in the power and authority of God as a unity. They were not given the authority to preach OR heal OR cast out demons. They were given authority to preach AND heal AND cast out demons.

The pattern of the ministry was not new. It was what they had seen demonstrated in the life and ministry of Jesus. All things found their unity in Him. He was the Word of God made flesh. When Jesus came out of the wilderness following the Temptation, He came preaching, "The time is fulfilled, the Kingdom of God is at hand; repent, and believe in the gospel." Mk 1:15   The Kingdom was at hand. It was in their midst. Men could touch it and be touched by it.

As the Kingdom of God was preached, the power of the Kingdom was manifest. It was manifest in the power to set men free by healing and casting out demons. The unity of the mission centered in the preaching. The healing and the casting out of demons followed. If they did not follow, the preacher was not in the authority of Jesus. The Kingdom of God was not being proclaimed as in our midst.

The early Christians had no problem with the proclamation. There was no doubt in their minds that they had been set free to walk in that Kingdom themselves. They had received the Holy Spirit and they were empowered from on high. They had received Him as the Spirit of adoption whereby they could say, "Abba, Father." as the Spirit bore witness with their spirits that they were the sons of God—heirs of God and joint heirs with Christ.

Fear was no longer a problem. They had no fear of death and hell. They rather had boldness toward God as they came to the throne of Grace to meet one who was their loving Father—not a tyrant who sought to punish and destroy them. The Ruler of the Kingdom was one who loved them. As they were born again in that love, they knew Him to be their Father. The death of the flesh did not mean the end of all things. It meant rather the completion of that adoption in the redemption of the body. They would live forever with the Father in a spiritual body fit to serve God in eternity.

They had no trouble understanding what Paul wrote to the Philippians. ". . . Christ will be honored in my body, whether by life or by death. For to me to live is Christ, to die is gain. If it is to be life in the flesh, that means fruitful labor for me. Yet which I shall choose I cannot tell. I am hard pressed between the two. My desire is to depart and to be with Christ, for that is far better. But to remain in the flesh is more necessary for your account." Phil 1:20-24 They lived to walk with Jesus—risen and present—whether in the flesh or out of the flesh mattered not. They sought to grow in His love, and to make that love known unto the whole world. When they encountered the risen Jesus, they were delivered from fear.

There were certainly Christians of this time who did not have such faith. There were some who even denied Jesus as they stood before the threat of the Roman courts. The fact that was true for all of them was that they lived in the family of God. They were surrounded by a crowd of witnesses—their brothers and sisters in Christ who nurtured them in the faith. They were a body of people who sought to find the grace to lay down their own lives in order that they might receive the life of Jesus. Martyrdom meant the immediate translation into God's Kingdom—the ultimate in their knowledge of deliverance.

They had one great advantage. Their decision to follow Jesus as Savior and Lord was not the result of social pressure to conform to what is nice. They did not make the choice just to please the family. Indeed the choice often meant alienation from the family of their blood kin. They were often disowned and cast out. If their family were Jewish, they were counted as dead.

Their decision was one of life and death. When they made their decision for Jesus, they united themselves with a new life in God's Kingdom. They also signed their own death warrants if they were ever brought before the Roman courts. They knew the power of the Kingdom in their lives. They preached the Kingdom in that power to deliver. They shared the Kingdom. People were healed and demons were cast out. Men were set free.

The decline in the power of the Church came as Christianity was accepted as the official religion of the Roman Empire. The situation was reversed. Christians were no longer under persecution for their faith. They were rather persecuted for not being Christians. From 310 AD the external pressure was to embrace Jesus Christ. Constantine had a vision of a cross in the sky with the words, "In hoc signo vinces"—in this sign conquer.

With the victory at Malvern Bridge, Constantine became the Emperor; and he proclaimed that the Christians were free from persecution by the government. The Christian faith became the official religion of the Empire, and the people were brought into the Church without any experience of the Lord. They were brought to baptism with little or no instruction in the faith. The faith of the body of Christians who had endured persecution was watered down by the many who were suddenly added to the body without any sense of the persecution that the others had endured.

The Council of Arles was called by the Emperor Constantine in 314 AD in order to regularize the order and organization of the Church. The Church had existed through the first three centuries under cover. No one knew exactly how she was ordered and held together as one body. It was to the amazement of the people that they found uniformity of order in bishops, priests, and deacons with the exception of the Church in Alexandria. That Church had the same order, but chose their bishops in a different way from the rest. As the organization became the center of the life of the Church, the charismatic power began to decline.

The decline was not immediate; and it was never quite complete. God had kept His 7,000 who have not bent the knee to Baal. He has kept His saints through all of history. His witness is constant in them, but the norm of charismatic power began to decline as the new converts were added by legislation rather than conversion. Up until this time, the sick were expected to be healed. The possessed and the mentally ill were expected to recover—to be delivered from bondage into the Kingdom of God.

The power was maintained only in those strange people called saints. They were set apart for God, and His power was still seen in their lives and in their ministries. Through them, God still exercised the power to heal the sick and cast out demons. They were the holy ones who had met Jesus, who had received the Holy Spirit, and who walked close to God.

Superstition became the norm of the people. They had lost the experience of the Kingdom. They did not know the King, and they were not given much knowledge about the Kingdom. It was presented as something that was only for the holy—the saints. The masses were to pay, pray, and obey. The realm of the Spirit was a realm of fear for them. Having lost the experience of Jesus and the power that was known in His Name, they returned to the incantations and the magic that man has sought to use from the dawn of time. Some even resorted to stealing the consecrated host from the celebration of the Holy Communion to wear as an amulet to protect them from evil.

The Church organization and leadership turned to the use of fear to maintain control. There was a new attitude born that saw manipulating people into obedience as the role of the Church rather than introducing them to the love of God in Jesus Christ. As the Roman Empire began to decline, the barbarians began to invade Rome from the north, and the whole world seemed to be coming unglued. The eternal city was fallen. The wrath of God was seen to be visited on the children of men; and the preaching itself changed.

When those who heard the proclamation failed to respond to its power, there was a shift from the Kingdom of God being at hand to the Kingdom of God being in the future. It was up in heaven. It was a reward for which men must be obedient and wait. There was a change in the focus of the sermon from the Kingdom of God to the behavior of man. If man was faithful in this life (and did all the Church asked of him), he would go to heaven when he died. The shift in the gospel was from experiencing the Kingdom to hoping for a Kingdom that could not be experienced in this life.

Faith, as it had been known in the early Church had been grounded in the experience of the people. Faith was a gift. God gave it by measure; but like the mustard seed, it did not grow until it fell into the ground. Once planted, it grew and yielded fruit—more experience that supported the growth of the faith that was put into the ground of life. In other words, when a Christian acted on his faith that God had given, the experience that followed told him that God was faithful. It was in this way that his faith grew. It is the same way that faith grows in the life of a Christian today. If it is never planted, it will never grow.

When the Kingdom of God is preached as being out of this world, faith must become trust in something else. If I believe that I am to go to heaven, but I have not yet experienced the Kingdom of God; I must have put my trust in the preacher or in the Bible or in the Church or in something other than my own experience of God. I may know God indirectly, but I am called to know Him face to face. In choosing to believe one of the intermediaries, I may believe someone with the authority of Christ; but I won't really know until I die. If I am wrong, that may be too late.

We will only grow faith when we plant faith. If we are trying to grow corn, we plant corn. If we are trying to grow beans, we plant beans. We plant what we want to grow. If we sow love, we will reap love. If we sow criticism, we will reap criticism. If we plant the faith God gives us, it will grow into abundant faith for life.

When the preaching began to find its center in a heaven that was up in the sky, it was also separated from healing and casting out demons. There were still a few who healed in obedience to Jesus, but the Church began to rationalize the passage from James which says, "Is any among you sick? Let him call for the elders of the Church, and let them pray over him, anointing him with oil in the name of the Lord; and the prayer of faith will save the sick man, and the Lord will raise him up, and if he has committed sins they will be forgiven." Ja 5:14-15

The meaning of that passage found a new interpretation. God was no longer healing the sick who were being anointed. The faith of the Church no longer offered the channel for His love to move. It must mean that God would save the sick man who was anointed after he died. After saving the sick man, God would raise him up in eternal life. With such an interpretation, the practice of anointing the sick with oil ceased to be seen as a healing sacrament and became a last rite. It was seen as the assurance of our forgiveness and our acceptance into heaven. Fortunately in recent years, unction has been restored to its proper meaning—anointing with oil to heal the sick.

The exorcist became one of the minor orders in the Church. In the beginning, no one was ordained as an exorcist. The effectiveness of the ministry was sign that he had been ordained by the Holy Spirit, and they did not lay hands on him. He was given permission by the bishop to exercise his ministry in the Church, and was called by the bishop when an exorcism was needed. The authority was given by the Holy Spirit. Permission was given by the bishop so that order might be kept in the Church.

As the ministry began to decline, the Church began to ordain men to the office of exorcist, and to give each one of them a book of exorcism rituals that they might use in the ministry. The Church was not able to confer the authority that the spirit alone can give; and the exorcists as a general rule did not have the power to cast out the demons that they encountered.

The resultant failure of the exorcists led to a tightening of the controls concerning exorcism. Today there is a large amount of red tape that one must go through in order to prove that someone is possessed and that exorcism is indicated; and then the Church will find an exorcist for the job at hand.

When I first found myself confronted by the possession of one of my people,

I knew nothing about the ministry of casting out demons. My seminary taught me nothing about it. I inquired of many of the priests in the area where I might find anything on the subject; and they knew nothing. I needed someone with authority to enable me to minister to a woman in deep need. I found none. I found a large number of men who would talk to me about counselling, but none who would talk to me about dealing with the problem that Jesus commissioned His Church to meet and solve.

There are those who believe that the reformation in 1517 was the beginning of the restoration of the Church to her former glory and power. The reformation cry of "solo gratia" or grace alone seemed to be a call back to a relationship to the risen Christ; but when the smoke had cleared, it was still faith in someone's teaching about doctrine or the Word. For the first time in the history of the Church, the Bible has been placed in the hands of the people; and they turned it into a weapon instead of a tool. Heaven was still in the future. The Kingdom of God was still known only to a few.

The leadership of the reformation did little to change the case of the people. The protestant leaders were just as certain of their doctrine as the Catholic leaders had been before. In the struggle to lay hold of the truth, they subected men to bondage even until death. In the battle following the reformation, there were about as many people killed by one side as the other.

The movement known as the renaissance came along about the same time as the reformation. Both were helped by the invention of the printing press. It was the dawn of what men have called the age of humanism in western civilization. Man became aware of himself as one who might control his own destiny. The Church had seen her witness torn asunder by the reformation. There was no longer a single source of Christian proclamation. The unity of the witness was lost in the multitude of voices clamoring to be heard as the true voice of God. Such a fragmented Church would be confronted and challenged by the voice and mind of man. The authority of the Church was no longer found in the gospel she preached or the ministry of power that had been learned from Jesus.

The authority of the Church had been changed. The Church no longer relied on the authority of Jesus—the enabling power of the Holy Spirit to set men free. She had been caught up in the political power that sought to save men's souls from the outside by imposing laws that would bring about his morality.

The same change in authority was noted in the way that the mentally ill were treated. They were confined to places that were inhuman. They were not treated with the authority of God's love to set them free; they were beaten and mistreated in the effort to drive out the demons that were believed to dwell within. It was no wonder that a person who had watched the authority of Jesus exchanged for the external authority of the old creation would believe that a demon might be driven out by physical punishment. Even today there have been cases of people who were beaten to death in an effort to set them free from the spirits that someone thought possessed them.

The inhuman treatment of the insane gave rise to the discipline of psychology. When the Church neglects the gospel, God often goes outside to raise up a body to bear His witness. Psychology did not find its roots in Christian love. Carl Jung, who was one of the more enlightened psychologists of this era, made the statement that psychology finds it roots in gnosticism in the ancient world. It was born in those men who sought to find God through wisdom instead of seeking wisdom through the revelation of God. It found its way through the ages through alchemy.

It was not practiced by the story-book alchemist who was forever trying to turn lead into gold. It was learned and taught by the ones who were seeking to find the secrets of life through wisdom. They were men who sought the hidden wisdom through the ages. They were men who used the occult since they did not embrace the revelation of God in Jesus Christ.

Those who began the work in the field of psychology had nothing but some of the higher wisdom of the old creation. They could speak of gentleness and love as do most of the world's religions; but they could not lay hold of the power to set men free in the Name of Jesus. They were, and are, limited to the same resources as the Jewish exorcists—to incantations and drugs. That was not much, but it was more than the Church of that day offered to deal with the problem of mental illness.

The element that was lacking in the Church was the experience of God. The failure to know God over the years had produced a double standard in the Church. There were the clergy who were supposed to be holy, and the laity who were not required to be as holy as the clergy. Along side of the whole futility of the Church were the saints, still living the normal Christian life in the power of the Spirit. The clergy had all of the answers, and the laity were supposed to park the brain at the baptismal font and obey the ones who were set in authority over them. The blind were leading the blind, and both fell into the ditch.

Theology took on the complicated task of apologizing for God—of making excuses for his not being active in His creation. The systems proved that man must stay in the Church if he was to have any hope for heaven. Those who left were certainly doomed to a hell of fire. This held true for both Catholic and Protestant.

To some extent, the Church is still in that condition, I do not find much difference between the Roman Catholic Church and the Pentecostal Holiness

Church—or any of the others for that matter. They all believe that they have the truth, and that all others are in error. What the priest or pastor says is the way it is. Anyone who disagrees is removed in one way or another. In some groups a member must submit every decision to his shepherd or pastor for this approval before the member can act. It is a far cry from the freedom of the early Christian Church where Jesus was THE Shepherd who still walked among the sheep; where the Holy Spirit ordained those whom He chose to do the work of ministry in the Body of Christ.

Where the proclamation of the gospel of the Kingdom of God is heard, men are still set free. The authority that was given by Jesus has never been withdrawn, it has simply been laid aside for the authority of the world. Jesus Christ is the same yesterday, today and forever. Where the gospel of God's Kingdom is preached as being at hand, the power of the gospel to heal and to cast out demons is also at hand. We are to come with the awareness that our truth is not yet complete, but that we are growing toward wholeness. Until all that we have is submitted to the fire of God's love, it cannot be pure.

We still have with us one error that is accepted as a presupposition of truth by most men. It is not new. It is as old as man himself. We believe, "If it works for me, it must be right for everyone else." We normally follow that with our next presupposition, "If you disagree with me, you must be wrong." Such presuppositions lead us to build our houses on the sand, and they destroy the integrity of the Body of Christ. That integrity can only be built on our confession of our error and God's truth in the sure knowledge that He is growing us up into the measure of the stature of the fullness of Christ.

Perhaps what we are trying to say might be best illustrated by a story I heard Jerre Mellili tell one day. He was talking about the way we messed up our handling of the differences that we have in the Body of Christ.

Jesus was walking down the road one day when a blind man was brought to Him seeking to be healed. Jesus spat on the ground and made some mud balls and put them on the man's eyes; and then He told the man to go and wash. The man did, and his sight was restored. The people were astounded. They were so impressed that they started the spit-on-the-ground-make-mud-balls-and-put-on-the-eyes-to-heal-the-blind church. As long as they remained true to their experience of Jesus' power in their lives, the blind were healed.

Farther down the road some people brought another blind man to Jesus to be healed. He laid His hands on the blind man and the blind man received his sight. The people were astounded. They were so impressed that they started the lay-hands-on-the-head-to-heal-the-blind-church. As long as they remained true to their experience of Jesus' power in their lives, the blind were healed.

One day one of the people from the first church was making a journey and happened by the other church. He decided to join them so that he might share his witness to the power of Jesus in his own home church. While he was there a blind man was brought to be healed, and as they were preparing to do what they had done so often before, the man stepped up to tell them what they were doing wrong. The result was that they got their eyes off Jesus, and onto the things that they were doing, and the power to heal was lost.

The story speaks well to our age when we are so quick to judge in the name of righteousness. We are so slow to support those we do not understand with either our prayers or our substance. As we have continued to fight one another in the name of Jesus, Satan has had a field day with the Church. He has led us to make the division of the mission to preach the gospel, to heal the sick and to cast out demons; and we have lost the Kingdom of God which is at hand. (Fortunately, God continues to find us.)

The Origin and Nature of Man

W HEN WE BEGIN our search to find out who we are and where we came from, we ask the same question as the psalmist. "Who is man that thou art mindful of him? or the son of man that thou visitest him? Thou madest him lower than the angels to crown him with glory and worship." Ps 8:4-5   It is apparent to the psalmist that we are shut into a world of time and space. It begins with our birth, and it ends with our death.

We are surrounded by a world of spirit that we cannot even see, and yet it seems to control our very destiny. The God of all the creation has reached down to establish man. He has made man His very own steward of creation. Man holds dominion over all things. In the midst of life and death, he is crowned with glory and worship. He is the crown of God's creation. The God who has created all things has shown him love and concern.

If we seek to find our origin through the genealogists—those who search their way through the mazes of family blood lines, we find that we come to an end before we come to an answer. There is really no way to penetrate the mists of the prehistoric ages with any certainty. We simply cannot climb back up our own family tree to our origin. We may know that somehow there must have been a beginning; but even if we follow the clarity of Genesis, we cannot know from whence Seth's wife came. We only know that we were born of our parents, and that in some way we must look to them for our contact with our origin.

That instinct which leads us to see our parents as the source of our life gives ground to one of man's oldest religions—that of ancestor worship. It begins with that sense of eternity that we receive from our parents. It issues in a great concern to bring forth children to carry on our blood line lest we be cut off from immortality. It does not truly enable us to deal with who we are and why we are here.

One of the most tragic figures that I have known was a man who was caught in this sort of web. It had been woven by his ancestors into a spotless image of family name. For our purposes we will call his John Stuart, although that was not his name in reality. He was a man whose family would not allow him to have any weaknesses. He could not confess any sins. He was a Stuart; and Stuarts were perfect. What few problems they had, they could handle without the help of anyone else—even God.

John was trapped. He knew that he had problems deep within—problems that were destroying him. He could not deal with his problems because he could not admit to anyone that he had them. He was forced to live in the family image. To break that image would be to destroy the line of his identity with immortality. It would be something closely akin to death. It is only as people like John are set free by the gospel of Jesus Christ that they can risk letting go of their family. When they realize that they are members of the eternal family of God, they are free to relinquish the blood lines of man from which they sprang.

Those who seek to find the answer in revolutionary theories leave man without any meaningful grasp of his origin. When the presentation of the theory has been made, they leave us with gaps and unexplained differences. Even worse, those who embrace evolution must realize that if it is true, nothing has any real or lasting purpose. We are rather the random product of an infinite variety of alternatives in a mechanical creation. As such we must see that we have come here by chance, and we will pass away into oblivion.

Those who do not know God often find it easier to say that God cannot be known than to seek him out. As long as their life is reasonably comfortable, they may feel that they have no need for God. The rub comes when life becomes so painful emotionally or physically that they begin to despair of living without a greater sense of purpose than they have. Until that point they want some explanation of their existence that will not bind them with any responsibility but that of making their own life comfortable. The trip from birth to death is short. They would make it as pleasant as they can; but please don't make it too difficult.

There is a story told about Charles Darwin, the author of the theory of evolution. He approached the Bishop of Lincoln one day, and said, "Surely, Bishop, you do not expect us to believe that Jonah was actually swallowed by a big fish."

The Bishop thought a bit and replied, "I do not know, Charles. When I get to heaven, I will ask him."

Darwin would not stop with such an answer, and so he pursued the bishop. "What if he is not in heaven?"

"In that event, you ask him."

The story indicated the futility of trying to lay hold of the truth of the universe or even its history by using man's reason alone. We must find another base for recognizing truth. The decision that we make about the basic realities of life is a faith decision. We will put our trust in something—in the Bible or in human reason—and our religion will come from that decision of faith. We will argue with others from our base of faith because we believe it to be true even though we cannot prove it to anyone but ourselves. I can verify my faith through my own experience; I cannot make you accept my experience unless you choose to do so.

The scriptures offer us another view of our origin that rests on another basis of faith. It is simply that God created the universe; and that he created man in His own image. God cares a great deal about man. He loves him with an unconditional love. He has even sent His only-begotten Son to put on our flesh so that we can know our origin and our destiny.

Jesus, God in our flesh, died for us that we might be raised up with Him into eternal life in God's Kingdom. As we are raised up with Him, we can begin to know that new creation that has been prepared for us. Those who would have me believe that we are evolving toward a goal of moral perfection in a world wherein carnal men will live in peace, must show me in the pages of history where they find their evidence. As I read history, I find on every page the same hatred and violence and murder as I find in the story of Cain and Abel.

I will not try to make anyone believe that there is a new way of life in a new creation; but I will invite anyone who desires to verify that truth to ask Jesus to reveal it to him. When we seek evidence of God's reality and love by trying out the revelation of God in the scriptures, we determine for ourselves that He is true. When we experience that reality, then we are able to build our own faith by receiving the witness of others also.

All of that means when we follow scripture, we know where we came from, and we know where we are going. That being true, we ought to take a look at the directions to see if we really want to go there. There are many who have decided that they do not want to go to hell, and they have chosen heaven by default. It would be good to know the nature of the Kingdom that we have chosen so that we might move toward it positively rather than backing in.

The story of the creation contains within it the account of man's fall. If we are to know ourselves, we must see the whole picture the scriptures present. "In the beginning God created the heavens and the earth . . . and God said, 'Let there be light . . .' " Gen 1:1   God spoke and the Word of God went forth to create. The Word of God is God Himself in the act of creating. When God speaks, His Word goes forth to accomplish the purpose of the speaker. The same theme is revisited by John as he opens his gospel. "In the begin-

ning was the Word . . . and the Word was made flesh and dwelt among us.''
Jn 1:1ff   He who brought forth the universe with a Word, brings forth a new
creation by the same Word.

As we continue reading in Genesis, we find that, ''God said, 'Let us make
man in our own image, after our likeness; and let them have dominion over
the fish of the seas, and over the birds of the air, and over the cattle, and
over all the earth, and over every creeping thing that creeps upon the earth.'
So God created man in his own image, in the image of God He created him;
male and female He created them.'' Gen 1:26-27

The image of God has remained a mystery; but whatever else it might mean,
it is not flesh and blood. Paul informs us that ''Flesh and blood shall not in-
herit the Kingdom of God.'' I Cor 15:50. We are also told, ''God is Spirit,
and those who worship Him must worship in spirit and in truth.'' Jn 4:24   Man
is not primarily a body that happens to have a spirit; he is a spirit that finds
expression through a body. Whatever maleness and femaleness might mean,
they find their roots in the spirit, and they manifest in the flesh. They are not
competitive and divisive of mankind; they are complementary and fulfilling
of one another.

As we move to the second chapter of Genesis, we find another view of the
creation. There is no conflict between the two stories; there are simply different images to tell the story. ''The Lord God formed man of dust from the
ground, and breathed into his nostrils the breath of life; and man became a
living being.'' Gen 2:7   We will find later that God initiates life in the new
creation in the same manner when Jesus appeared to the disciples after being
raised from the dead. ''He breathed on them and said, 'Receive the Holy Spirit
. . .' '' Jn 20:22

After God created man, he placed him in Eden to till the soil and to keep
it. God planted all of the vegetation; and in the midst of the garden, He planted
the tree of knowledge of good and evil. Adam, the man, could eat freely of
all of the fruit of the garden except this one tree. God assured him that the
day he ate of that tree, he would surely die.

God saw further that it was not good for man to live alone; and so He created
all of the animals, and He brought them to the man to see what he would name
them. It was in the naming of the animals that man established his dominion
over them. After all of the animals had been brought to the man, it was found
that none of them was suitable as a helpmate for him.

''So the Lord God caused a deep sleep to fall upon the man, and while he
slept, he took one of his ribs and closed up its place with flesh; and the rib
which the Lord God had taken from the man he made into a woman and brought
her to the man.'' Gen 2:21-22   The woman was not just another animal. She

was human as he was human. He had never seen such a creature before, but the moment he saw her, he knew that she was for him. She was the creation of God that would complete his life and make him whole.

"This at last is bone of my bone and flesh of my flesh; she will be called woman because she has been taken out of man." Gen 2:23   She was everything that Adam had been looking for among the other animals. She was that gift that made man whole as the two were made one flesh. There is an old rabbinic saying that deals with this account of the creation of man and woman. "The Lord God did not create woman from man's head that she might be over him, nor from his feet that he might walk upon her; but from his side that she might stand next to him, from under his arm that he might protect her, close to his heart that he might love her."

They were both naked, and they were not ashamed. They were as the rest of the animal kingdom. They had no knowledge of good and evil; they had no moral sense. Their behavior grew out of the instincts with which they had been programmed by the Creator. They made no moral choices. They did not even have the tools to make a moral chioce if they had been faced with one. They were obedient to God as the animals were. They were obedient to the instincts within them as the birds which know to fly south for the winter or a bear that knows when to hibernate. It was simply the way God had put them together.

The serpent came to tempt Eve, the woman. Some point out that she had a built-in alibi. God had given the commandment not to eat the forbidden fruit to Adam before He created Eve. As far as we know, God had not told her directly; but as the conversation was engaged, it became evident that someone had told her. She was able to state clearly that if they ate of the fruit, they would surely die.

The serpent used what he always uses to get to people. He used half truths. "God knows that when you eat of it, you will be like God's knowing good and evil," is the truth. "You shall not surely die." is the lie. Yet who among us can condemn Eve for her choice? Is not that what we seek when we decide to follow Jesus in order to become like Him?

They took the fruit, and they ate it, and their eyes were opened, and they realized that they were naked. It is at this point that we first find the creation of man as we know him. We find man with a moral sense that drives him to keep himself covered in some way. Shame is a uniquely human experience which we find even in the most primative cultures. The reaction of Adam and Eve was to sew fig leaves together and make aprons to cover their nakedness.

When God came to walk in the cool of the day, Adam and Eve hid because they were afraid. For the first time they realized that there was a good and an evil. When they were confronted with their disobedience, they instituted the universal human practice of self justification. Adam blamed Eve in an effort to clear himself of guilt. Eve blamed the serpent, and the serpent had to stand and take it because there was no one else in the situation. It is notable that shifting the blame to someone else did not alter the consequences. It still does not alter the consequences even though it is one of our more popular pastimes today.

It is notable also that God continued to love them. It was necessary to drive them out of the garden to fulfill the plan of God. He did not intend to let them take of the fruit of the tree of life and eat and live forever. (We shall see later that God did allow man to take the fruit, but God gives the fruit as a gift in Jesus Christ. It is He who is the true fruit of life borne on the tree which was His cross.) Before he drove them out of the garden, God made them coats of skins to clothe them. This is the first record of blood being shed for man.

The scene closes with the cherubim being placed at the gate of the garden with a flaming sword that turns in every direction. God made certain that man could not take the Kingdom by force. The gift of eternal life is not to be grasped but received on God's terms and by God's initiative. That will be a part of the reconciliation that God had already prepared for man in Jesus Christ.

Adam's relationship to God prior to the fall was one of justice. God did all that He was supposed to do; and Adam did all he was supposed to do. Everything was fair. Each got what he deserved from the relationship. Perhaps this accounts for that haunting dream of man that leads him to feel that somewhere there is something called justice. Somewhere there is a place where things are fair—a place where man can earn and deserve the salvation that he seeks.

After the fall, justice was not what man needed. The last thing that he could use was what he deserved. He could no longer claim that he deserved life; he forfeited that claim when he chose to eat the forbidden fruit. Now he needed mercy.

There are many who regret the fall of man. There are many Christians who yearn for a return to Eden. They want to be able to enter into a justice relationship with God so they can merit their salvation. They want to live a life in the garden where the work seems easy, and no decisions have to be made. They wish to return to the relationship of justice, but that is not what God has in mind for us.

Prior to the fall, there was no way for man to know the true nature of God. As long as man held up his end of the bargain, he received justice from God; and he knew God to be just. When he fell, and God reached out across the gulf to show His concern for man; then man could see God's love as something greater than justice. God could not reveal His love until man no longer deserved what he was given. The fall must have been within the scope of God's purpose. It was essential to the revelation of His primary characteristic—the very substance of His being.

We should never lament the fall of man. We should rather rejoice that God had something better in mind for man than primal innocence in the garden. There was no moral capacity in man who only reacted to the programming of his instincts. He could make no choices of the will; he could simply react to the world in which he lived, and the God who created it. It was after the fall that we received the capacity to know and to choose. We are not to look back; we are to look forward into the Kingdom of God. We have been made God's children in His love revealed in Jesus Christ. We are now heirs of God and joint heirs with Christ.

Let us take another look at the temptation of Eve. She did not seek to do something wrong. She sought to do the right thing in the wrong way. If there is anything wrong in seeking to be like God, then we are all guilty. It is precisely that goal to which we are called as Christians. Jesus came to put on our humanity so that we might put on His divinity. The very seeds of our becoming like God are in the temptation of Eve and the fall of man.

The grave error of Eve was pride and presumption. She was going to reach out and grasp that which God had not yet offered. She was going to take the Kingdom on her own initiative. Jesus' life showed us a better way as Paul relates, "Have this mind among yourselves, which you have in Christ Jesus, who, though he was in the form of God, did not count equality with God a thing to be grasped. But emptied Himself, taking the form of a servant, being born in the likeness of men. And being found in human form he humbled himself and became obedient unto death, even death on a cross. THEREFORE GOD HAS HIGHLY EXALTED HIM and bestowed on him the name that is above every name, that at the name of Jesus, every knee shall bow in heaven and on earth and under the earth, and every tongue confess that Jesus Christ is Lord, to the glory of God the Father." Phil 2:5-11

The difference is clear. Adam and Eve were not in the form of God, and yet they reached out to grasp that equality with God which would have been robbery for them. They tried to take what was not theirs. Jesus was in the form of God, but when He put on human flesh, He emptied Himself so the Father would have the initiative in exalting Him. It would not have been robbery for Jesus to do what Adam and Eve tried; it was His right. He emptied Himself so that we might see the example of His humility for our lives.

The revelation of God comes to us through both Adam and Jesus. The experience of Adam shows us that we cannot seize the Kingdom of God by force.

The cherubim with the flaming sword will see to that. Jesus' example shows us that we do not have to seize the Kingdom by force; God shall give it to us by His own initiative. "Fear not little flock, for it is your Father's good pleasure to give you the Kingdom." Lk 12:32   We receive as a gift that which we cannot take by force or guile. It is also evident that "God resisteth the proud and giveth grace to the humble." I Pet 5:5

When a mother finds her child with his hand in the cookie jar, she may well slap his wrist (or some other part of the anatomy). It does not necessarily mean that she is mad with the child. It certainly does not mean that she does not intend for the child to have food to eat. She is simply telling the child to ask before he takes so that he might be able to receive instead. She is trying to teach him that it is better to receive what is prepared for you than to try to take what you want. When Eve reached out to take the fruit of the tree of knowledge of good and evil, she got her wrist slapped because she was trying to steal God's initiative.

Adam and Eve interpreted God's action in an entirely different way. They saw it as punishment for something that they had done wrong. They saw it as a loss of security and ease of living—as separation from God. I imagine they were much like us, and they soon forgot that they were the ones who had hidden from God. God had not hidden from them. As long as man continues to live in fear of God, he will continue to hide from Him.

I know in my own experience I was reluctant to come to God. I had been threatened with hell and punishment. In His Name, people had demanded things I could not give. I was invited to be like them to avoid the wrath of God. They didn't seem very happy, and so I ran and hid. At least I tried to hide from God until I heard of His love for me. As I came to know Him, I realized the error that had been taught me "for my own good."

I came to realize that even His wrath was His love. It was the fire of His love poured out to consume the Sin in me. It was His power purging out my corruption to establish His incorruption. God's wrath is not to be avoided but embraced. It is not for our punishment but for our purification. Whatever God has willed for us is better than anything that we could will for ourselves. He has even turned death into victory.

The death that entered the scene in Eden was a part of the promise. It was not punishment; it was an essential step that we all must take as we move toward the Kingdom of God. It is a source of sorrow to many who do not want to die; but it is a necessary fact if we are to know God to be both just and loving. As we look further at God's revelation, we see that death is necessary for us to enter eternal life through resurrection in Jesus Christ.

It is very much as God has shown us in nature. If a caterpillar does not spin a cocoon and die as a worm, he will never emerge as a butterfly. That is why the butterfly is a symbol of the resurrection. We are not called to "avoid death at all costs." That is the prayer of those who do not know God. We are called to embrace death so that God's absolute justice might be satisfied in us. We are called to resurrection life in Jesus so that God's eternal love might be satisfied.

The remedy for the sickness that struck man and caused the fall was prepared long before the plague. God had prepared the answer before the question was asked. "You know that you were ransomed from the futile ways inherited from your fathers, not with perishable things such as gold and silver, but with the precious blood of Jesus Christ, like that of a lamb without blemish or spot. He was destined before the foundation of the world but was made manifest at the end of the times for your sake." I Pet 1:18-20

In this light we see man as the beloved of God. He is the creation that God called into being through His Word. He has only one conceivable purpose before God. He was created so that God would have someone to love. God did not create man to love in some general way. He made each of us a particular expression of man, and He loves each of us in a particular way. When we were baptized, we did not receive a number. We received a name by which we are called in the family of God. He loves each one of us unconditionally, and He calls us each by name.

We are called to praise God; but God could receive praise from someone else, if I do not praise Him. Certainly we are called to serve God; but God would be served without my existence. The only thing that God could not do without me is have someone named Alfred Lee to love. Even as I respond to that love with praise and service, I find that God's love enables me to receive from Him. He gives Himself to me so that I might have love to return to Him and give to others. "This is love, not that we loved God, but that God first loved us and gave himself for us . . ." I Jn 4:10

That purpose for our creation is a conclusion we come to only after we have exhausted every means of justifying ourselves. We first try to find some basis for staking our claim in the Kingdom of God. We try to find a way to believe that we deserve a place. I used to seek to maintain a moral norm that I thought was better than half of the people because I thought that God would accept at least half of us in heaven. If I kept myself better than half of the people, then I would deserve a place in heaven. I have come to believe that the lot assignments have already been made. It simply remains to be seen how we will build on them.

It is the struggle of man to justify himself that makes the gospel good news.

When we come to the end of our string, we are open for God to move in with His grace to do that which we cannot do. Most of us are familiar with the statement from Ephesians, ''By grace you have been saved through faith; and this is not of your own doing, it is a gift of God—not because of works, lest any man should boast.'' Eph 2:8-9

After reciting that bit of truth, we have a tendency to turn to our brethren in the faith and require of them some sort of minimum standard of behavior. If they do not meet our standard, we are prone to unchurch them. We condemn them as not being Christians by virtue of their behavior. Until we see that we cannot meet even a minimum standard without grace, we will fail to believe what we profess to be our faith, and we will be striving with the wind.

All men are born in Sin. They are not able to live in the righteousness of God. Whether or not they are totally depraved, we can say without a doubt that we are totally inadequate. There is no way in which we can care for ourselves or serve anyone else as we come into the world. We are to understand that God does not impute guilt to us as we are willing to receive the forgiveness that has been given us in Jesus. We cannot even condemn ourselves.

Original Sin is not the same as original guilt. It is our inability to reach the image of perfection that haunts us. It is an inner Sin that God has promised to deal with in each of us. The prophet Jeremiah understood this dilemma, and he prophesied, ''Behold the days are coming says the Lord, when I will make a new covenant with the house of Israel and the house of Judah . . . I will put my law within them, and I will write it upon their hearts; and I will be their God and they will be my people . . . for they shall all know me from the least to the greatest, says the Lord; for I will forgive their iniquity, and I will remember their sin no more.'' Jer 31:31f

Original Sin stems from the origin of the human race as we know it. It does not mean that we carry the guilt for Adam's disobedience. It means that we are born into the same condition—we have a capacity for knowing good and evil. We sense that in some way we should be better than we are. We feel that if we just tried a little harder, we could make it. The whole creation has been subjected to bondage. We are born into that bondage to the flesh.

Original Sin is dealt with through regeneration. It is not a matter of excusing weakness. It is a matter of destroying weakness, and making us whole. The new creation which is in God's love results when the power of God reprograms our hearts and minds so that the choices we make will naturally be in accord with God's will. It is the particular step that we must take that we might receive the mind of Christ.

When man begins to recognize his inability to cope out of his own strength and wisdom, he looks for a Messiah. There are many messiahs in the world that do not come from God. They present themselves to us through their followers, and they promise to enable us to cope with life as we meet it. Alcohol, drugs, sex, money, and power are all candidates today; but none of them can deliver man from his bondage.

Man has looked for one who would come along and straighten out the world. He looks for some power to make the world a fit and safe place to live. God has sent His Messiah not to clean up the world, but to clean up the people who are willing to be changed. It is significant that Jesus did not ride into Rome on an ass and a colt, the foal of an ass; He rode into Jerusalem, the holy city. He did not go to clean up the palace; He went to cleanse the Temple that was the dwelling place of God on earth. He seeks to build a Temple that is a fit place for Him to live. He has sent Jesus to make us a Temple of flesh in which He can dwell on earth, and we might be prepared to dwell with Him in heaven.

"What is man that thou art mindful of him? and the son of man that thou visitest him?" When we consider that the God of the whole universe has condescended to come to earth to suffer for us that we might know His love, it is awesome. He has made us lower than the angels; but He has chosen the inadequate, the weak, and the inept to be transformed into the body of His grace.

We struggle with our encounter with good and evil. We seek to know more fully the will of God in particular circumstances in our lives. We find when we strive in our own power to deal with evil, we are defeated. We may win a battle from time to time; but Satan will win the war. It is only when we turn to the power and authority of the cross, and the Name of Jesus who was crucified for us that we find the power that is able to deliver us from evil. It matters little whether we are good or bad; we must all be made new.

The Problem of Evil

THE PROBLEM OF EVIL has been a mystery to man. We know that it is there because we have the capacity to know good and evil. We cannot agree on the definition of what is actually good and what is actually evil. Nearly all of the atrocities that have happened in the history of the world were committed because someone thought that they were good. In the final analysis we can only agree on the fact that there is good and there is evil.

Most Christians have been taught that all good is from God and all evil is from Satan. That makes the issue very simple for us, but it raises some questions. The Church has proclaimed that God has overcome Satan. The victory was won in the cross of Christ wherein we were redeemed by the blood of Jesus. If the victory was truly won, then why do we believe that God and Satan are still at war within the creation? Why is it not finished as Jesus said from the cross?

Those who question the Christian faith ask, "If God is really good, and if God has beaten Satan, why doesn't evil cease?" "If God has power over Satan and does not destroy him, then God is as evil as the Satan He allows to continue." If we are to deal with the objections that others raise to the faith, then we must answer their questions. I know that if I could eliminate Satan from the scene, and in so doing eliminate all evil; I would certainly do it. If I did not, I would be giving my own assent to that evil.

That is not a pleasant thing to think about God, but that is the evidence by which we are confronted. If our proclamation is true—that God is love—then we must say that God uses such evil as there is in the world for good. That is certainly the case in Joseph's life. When his brothers sold him into slavery to the Midianite traders, they meant it to him for evil. God used it for good. Joseph saw that reality. "God sent me before you to preserve for you a remnant on earth, and to keep alive for you many survivors. So it was not you who sent me here but God . . ." Gen 45:7-8 Paul says much the same thing in different words, "All things work together for good to those who love God, to those who are called according to his purpose." Rm 8:28

Does that mean that the things we perceive as being evil are not really evil? Not at all. If there were no evil in the world, the cross of Jesus would be a mockery. He died that we might be set free from the evil one. We were locked into our Sin. We did not and could not know God. When we say that "God was in Christ reconciling the world unto himself," II Cor 5:19 we are saying that God has taken care of our Sin which separates us from Him. He no longer counts our transgressions against us. God has acted to put an end to our separation when we choose to receive the gift.

John tells us that Jesus was manifested in order that "He might destroy the works of the devil." I Jn 3:8   He did not come to destroy the devil, but what the devil was doing. When the devil brings us into bondage to Sin, we deserve to die that the justice of God might be fulfilled. Jesus did not just take away our guilt. He forgives our Sins not by excusing them but by our death in His death, and our new life in His resurrection. The old man is gone, and the new man has not sinned.

If I were guilty of a crime that demanded a death penalty, I would deserve to die in the gas chamber or electric chair or in some other manner. When I had been put to death, justice would be served. My debt would be paid. If by some miracle, I was raised from death; then I would no longer deserve death. I would be free. Our forgiveness of Sin by Jesus follows much the same pattern. We receive what we deserve when we are buried with Christ in His death. When we are raised, we are not the same person who was in Sin unto death. We are a new creation.

When Jesus was raised from the dead, He became the first-fruit of God's new creation—He was the first-born of many brethren. The works of the devil are destroyed in me when I die with Him; and I am translated into the Kingdom of God as a new creature in a new creation. Satan has no place in the new Kingdom. He can no longer stand before the throne of God day and night accusing us. When we leave the old and enter the new we are out of reach. When we are born again into the new creation, we begin to live in two creations—both the old and the new.

The two are not the same. Each creation has its own nature, and each has its own set of rules. The old creation was made to pass away. It is subject to vanity and corruption. That is where we begin our life. The new creation is eternal. It is set free from all bondage. That is where we find our eternal life. In passing from the old to the new our sins are forgiven. They cannot exist in the new.

Paul was very concerned that the Galatian Church realize this truth. They had been set free in Jesus Christ by the power of the gospel. They had known the freedom of the Holy Spirit in their lives; but some came with human reason who turned their eyes from the risen Christ to their own behavior. They began to focus their attention on what they had to do to hold fast their salvation. They had been given the Spirit that they might walk in the Spirit; but they were reasoned back into a set of rules. They were told that if they were going to live by the grace of God, they had to do something about it themselves. The law was God's will, and if they really loved Him they would keep it. The Judaisers who sought to bring the law to the Galatian Church constrained them to be both circumcised and to keep the rest of the law.

The situation was very similar to an experience I had with a woman that we will call Sally. She was an alcoholic. She further complicated her drinking with loose living in her sexual life. For some people in the world this might be called high living, but for Sally it was hell. When she came to me, she was delighted to find that God might love her in spite of the things that she had done. We prayed with her to receive Jesus as her Lord and Savior; and we asked that He fill her with the Holy Spirit. The change in her life was apparent from that very day. We continued to pray with her for deliverance and for inner healing, and she made her confession and received God's absolution. After that she began to find freedom from her old life patterns.

She did well until someone began to tell her what SHE had to do. Up until that time, she let God do for her what she could not do for herself. When she was free, her Christian friends pointed out that she needed to do something for God. The effort threw her back to her own resources, and it lasted very few days. When she returned to her old resources, she returned to her old bondage to fear and the old patterns of life from which God had set her free.

Sally went through cycles of offering her problems to God and getting free, and then trying to do something for God and falling back into the old patterns. She was fine as long as she rested in the power of God; when she tried to go back to her own strength, she fell. Strangely enough, it was not the power of Satan in the flesh that caused her to fall; but the power of Satan working through those who called themselves her Christian friends. He worked through those who kept trying to make her "keep the law that they imposed upon her."

The work of the devil is not always open and visible; it is often cloaked in some form of righteousness. It sounds very reasonable to me when someone says, "God has done so much for me, I feel that I must do something for Him." We then set about to see what will keep us in His good graces. The truth is that we cannot do anything good without God being at the root of the matter. Jesus taught us in the parable of the vine and the branches, "I am the vine and you are the branches. He who abides in me, and I in him, he it is that bears much fruit, for apart from me you can do nothing.'' Jn 15:5   All that we can do for God is allow Him to bring forth fruit in us and through us. I can allow Him to prune me, and nourish me, and give me life.

Jesus has not called us to resurrection without death. There are many who would like to avoid dying to their world and their things. They would like to slip into the new creation and take the best of the old along with them. They give up their life to the extent that they cannot handle it; but they hold fast to what they can handle. They are much like the Jews with the Temple worship; it was the best they knew so it must be good enough for God.

The Christian life is summed up by Paul in the last chapter of Galatians. ''In Christ Jesus neither circumcision availeth anything nor uncircumcision, but a new creature. Peace and mercy be upon all who walk by this rule, upon the Israel of God.'' Gal 6:15-16   The rule again is not whether we are good or bad, but we must be made new if we are to live in the Kingdom.

It would seem to me that the presence of the new creation gives us a new way to think about good and evil. The dualism is no longer with us in terms of God against Satan. It is between the law and the gospel; between justice and love; between the old creation and the new. Perhaps we can see that Satan is just a pawn of God. He is the tempter, the accuser, the one to whom it is given to destroy the flesh; but all of his evil cannot take away the people of God from His hand. He is allowed to do nothing that cannot be redeemed and turned to good by the creative power of God's love. He becomes rather the goad that drives us out of the old creation into the new where God might perfect us—''That he might present us to himself a glorious church, not having spot or wrinkle, or any such thing; but that it should be holy and without blemish.'' Eph 5:27

THE OLD CREATION

When I decided to work toward my masters degree, I chose to write my thesis on exorcism. I had become involved in the ministry, and I wanted to know more about how it had been used in the very early days of the Church. I wanted to know why it had fallen into disuse. I had to begin with the foundation—the Old Testament. Our Christian roots did not spring from the air. They sprang from the root of Jesse—the new grew out of the old.

I expected to find what I had always heard to be true. I thought I would find that there was a war going between Satan and God. God had created him as an angel of light. He had rebelled against God because he was proud. In his rebellion, he had fallen into enmity with God. That was the story that I had heard from most of those who took God seriously, and who looked upon Satan as something more than a superstition.

When I began to read the Old Testament, that was not what I found at all. I was amazed to find that God was the author of both good and evil. He was the Creator of all things. God sent both sickness and healing. He sent both drought and famine; rain and plenty. He did pretty much what He wanted to do. There were other gods, but they were pawns in the hands of Yahweh. He alone was the great God of gods who used nations that did not know Him as His servants.

The people of that day believed that every nation had a god of its own, and the king of the nation was the manifestation of the diety that really pulled the strings. Wars were fought by men, but it was the gods who determined the outcome. Isaiah uses this kind of imagery that speaks of king and god together when he pronounces the doom of the king of Babylon. The king sought to exalt himself above the heavens just as his forbears had in trying to build the great tower of Babel. Yahweh saw to it that he would go down into the pit. The gods of Babylon, or any other nation, were in power only as long as Yahweh permitted.

The great rebellion against God in the Old Testament seems to have issued from His own people. They were the only ones who had contact with him. They were the only ones who could truly rebel. Satan seemed to have access to the throne room with the sons of God. At least that is where we find him in the Book of Job. He had a job to do, and he did it well. He was not always right in his evaluation of people since he could not read their hearts as God could. He made a mistake in his judgment of Job, but he was still subject to God and stayed within the limits set. He took no more than he was authorized to take.

We meet Satan again in Zechariah. He had Joshua in tow; and it seemed that Joshua deserved what he was getting. His garments were filthy, which was sinful for a priest. Likely his life style lacked a little also. Satan had done his job well. Joshua was reaping what he had sown, and he stood in his rightful place beside Satan. "The Lord said to Satan, 'The Lord rebuke thee, O Satan; even the Lord that hath chosen Jerusalem rebuke thee; is this not a brand snatched out of the fire?' " Zech 3:2

It was not that Satan had taken something that was not his, or that he fought to keep something that the Lord wanted. He was doing his job when he was confronted by the command, and he gave up Joshua because the Lord had something else in mind. God had decided to redeem the priest and purify him that the worship of the Temple in Jerusalem might be restored to righteousness. There was no argument; there was no fight; there was a simple compliance with the words which the Lord had spoken. I find it much the same way in exorcisms today. There is no need to shout or fight. It is the authority of God that gets the job done.

God created the serpent and placed him in the garden. He supplied him with the half truths to tempt Eve. He did his job well; both Adam and Eve fell for it. I have always assumed that since disobedience was involved in the fall that God did not intend for it to happen. I have come to believe otherwise, as we pointed out in the last chapter. It is harder for me to believe that God made a mistake than it is for me to believe that He intended the fall. It is even harder for me to believe that God would prepare a remedy for something that was not going to happen.

We do not see that remedy in the Old Testament, but we see the advance signs of it. We hear the prophecy of the one who is to come. We hear the prophecy of the Day of the Lord when God will come to restore peace on the earth and to all of its inhabitants. We hear the prophecy of the servants by whose stripes we are healed. The prophets knew that God alone could set straight the mess that men had made of the world. They knew that he would one day come to accomplish His will on earth as in heaven.

Until the coming of Jesus, Satan seems not so much an enemy of God as a servant of God who can in no way be called a servant of man. He is the goad that makes life so miserable in the old creation that we are driven to the new. He is the owner of the hog pen where the prodigal sons of God realize that the Father has better things for His servants than the world has for her children. He is the reminder that we cannot build the kingdom of self and maintain it where others are trying to do the same thing.

Satan's work in God's plan of salvation is not attractive, and it certainly has no future, but I for one am glad that God set it up this way. Without the goad, I would become complacent with my growth. I would allow God to deal with all of the things I was not able to handle; but I would hold fast to the things that I could. Satan is given the job of destroying the flesh; he has never let me get comfortable enough to sit still. He contributes nothing positive to our life, but his negative, destructive work drives us to the positive as God calls us to Himself.

It is interesting to note that Satan is not responsible for all of the evil spirits in the Old Testament. As a matter of fact, he seems to have been responsible for none of them. When God sent Saul to destroy the Amalekites, Saul decided that he had a better idea. He did not destroy all of the animals, and he did not kill Agag, the king. God had given him plan A, Saul's reason had led him to execute plan B. That constituted rebellion against God; and that is the same as witchcraft—it is trying to get God to change His will so that He might do our will.

For that disobedience, God rejected Saul from being king, and David was anointed by Samuel. When David was anointed, the spirit of the Lord rested upon him. "But the Spirit of the Lord departed from Saul, and an evil spirit FROM THE LORD troubled him. And Saul's servants said to him, 'Behold now, an evil spirit from God troubleth thee.' " I Sam 16:14-15   For whatever reason God sent the evil spirit to Saul, it was God that sent it. He used it to teach Saul that there is no substitute for obedience to the living God; and He used it to get David into Saul's court.

The servants seemed to be aware of how to deal with the evil spirits of that day. They suggested to Saul that he find someone who was skilled with a harp to play and sing. The dispelling of the evil spirit came through incantation. David was found to be skilled with the harp. When he was brought in to play for Saul, Saul loved him very much. When David played, "Saul was refreshed and well, and the evil spirit departed from him." I Sam 16:23   The deliverance was not lasting, the evil spirit continued to return.

Elsewhere we find another illustration of God being the author of both good and evil. When Ahab and Jehoshaphat decided to go up and fight the Syrians, the prophets were brought forth to prophesy. When the prophets of Israel came to speak their prophesies, "Zedekiah made him horns of iron; and he said, 'Thus saith the Lord, with these shalt thou push the Syrians, until thou have consumed them.' " I Ki 22:11   All of the other prophets of Israel concurred that the two kings should go up to Ramoth-gilead where they would win the day.

Jehoshaphat was not satisfied with the prophets of Israel, and asked if there were a prophet of the Lord left in the land. It was then that they sent for Michaiah. Ahab did not want to hear him because he never said anything good about Ahab. When he arrived, the question was asked, "Shall we go up or not?"

Ahab had not asked for a word from the Lord, and Michaiah did not bother to give him one. His answer was short and sweet, "Go, and prosper; for the Lord shall deliver it into the hand of the king."

Ahab could not believe the good words that the prophet spoke concerning him; and so he rephrased his question and made it a command. "I adjure thee that thou tell me nothing but what is true in the name of the Lord."

That changed the question entirely. The question was no more addressed to the man but to the prophet in the man. "And he said, 'I saw all Israel scattered upon the hills, as sheep that have not a shepherd;' and the Lord said, 'These have no master; let them return every man to his house in peace.' " That was not enough as the prophet continued to speak, "Hear thou therefore the word of the Lord; I saw the Lord sitting on his throne, and all the host of heaven standing by him on his right hand and on his left. And the Lord said, 'Who shall persuade Ahab, that he may go up and fall at Ramoth-gilead?' And one said on this manner and another said on that manner. And there came forth a spirit, and stood before the Lord, and said, 'I will persuade him.' And the Lord said unto him, 'Wherewith?' And he said 'I will go forth, and I will be a lying spirit in the mouth of all his prophets.' And he said, 'Thou shalt persuade him, and prevail also; go forth, and do so.' " I Ki 22:19-23

It would seem that there was no conflict between God and the lying spirit. The conflict was between God and Ahab. In every instance the people of Israel and Judah are shown that Yahweh is greater than every other god or spirit. The presence of the other spirits in the world allow God's people the opportunity to try God and to try the spirits so that they might know the truth. This is the purpose of the recorded history of Israel. It points out the failure of the people as they turned away from Yahweh to serve the other gods. Their successes were recorded as gifts that issued from repentence as they turned back to the God who had called them to be His own.

The people of Israel and Judah alone had access to God through the prophets. They were His people because He had called them His own. He had called them from nothing to make them a great nation as long as they walked in His will. He did not give them the revelation of His presence and power so they could keep it for themselves. He had called them to be a light unto the nations, "I will also give thee for a light unto the gentiles, that thou mayest be my salvation unto the ends of the earth." Isa 49:6   There will be a day when all men shall bend their knee to God, ". . . unto me every knee shall bow, every tongue shall swear." Isa 45:23

It is the same theme that Zechariah picks up as he prophesies "In those days it shall come to pass, that ten men out of all languages of the nations even shall take hold of the skirt of him that is a Jew saying, 'we will go with you; for we have heard that God is with you . . .' " Zech 8:23

This is the nature of the Old Testament. God used both good and evil to accomplish His own will and purpose in the people He had called to be His own. Here was no conflict between God and the spirits. God was sovereign over all of the gods and the spirits. The old creation was made to pass away—the new is another matter.

THE NEW CREATION

Things began to change in the New Testament, but the change is not one that we might think at first. Since there was not any conflict in the old creation between God and Satan, why should there be any in the new? Is not God Almighty? The answers come to us as we examine the new in the light of the old.

When Jesus was baptized, He came up out of the water and the Holy Spirit descended on Him like a dove, and a voice from heaven said, "You are my beloved son in whom I am well pleased." Mk 1:11   It would seem then that Jesus would have been sheltered from Satan after that. We find instead that the Spirit cast Jesus out into the wilderness to be tempted by the devil.

This temptation was the prelude to the rest of Jesus' ministry. It was in this encounter with Satan that we see the nature of His ministry revealed as a new reality at the spiritual level. There was something more than the law and the prophets with their demands that men could not fulfill. The course of action was set for the inbreaking of a NEW creation. It was in the area of the temptations that the decisions were made clear. The new creation would be very different from the old. The initiative would no longer come from the outside through the written code, but from the inside as the prophet had spoken—the law written upon the heart. These are the directions that had to be determined before the ministry could begin.

The temptation was threefold. Jesus was tempted to make bread from stone; to use the authority of the world to bring in the Kingdom of God. If we think in terms of the world, these don't sound bad at all. There is nothing wrong with feeding the hungry; great effort has been put forth by the Church to do just that. There is nothing wrong with living in peace in the world; the Church has always urged the cessation of war in the world. There is nothing wrong with signs and wonders; the Church has always pointed to the saints in whose lives they occur. As a matter of fact, these are the areas of life where the Church and the world can agree.

Satan did not tempt Jesus to do evil as we understand evil. He tempted Jesus to do good; but it was good out of order. There was no temptation to destroy anyone or anything. He tempted Jesus to bring in the Kingdom of God in the wrong way. Jesus did not react to Satan by casting him into the pit. He simply responded by telling him that things would be done under the direction of God and not the world. There was a new world coming that would be different from the old. The difference would be in the fabric of the new creation set free from sin and death. Each one of the temptations had a proper response as the confrontation between the two continued.

The first of the temptations was one which speaks to the experience of many in the world who suffer from hunger. ''If you are the Son of God, command these stones to become bread.'' Satan's temptation is twofold. Jesus, in His humanity was hungry after fasting forty days; but even greater was the need of humanity for food to nourish their starving bodies.

Jesus' response was direct and to the point, ''Man shall not live by bread alone, but by every word of God.'' Lk 4:4 Later in His ministry, when the people He taught had need for bread, He fed them. He fed them in a miraculous way when He took the offering of bread and fish that was so inadequate and made it more than enough for the crowd. He fed them first with the teaching of the Kingdom; and then with the bread for the body. Jesus knew that man could not be satisfied with the meeting of his material needs alone.

When I was a child, I was taught by the authorities in our education system that man had only three basic needs—food, clothing and shelter. As I grew up, I found they were wrong. They were in bondage to the blindness of the old creation which sees man only from the outside. They did not know that love was essential to our wholeness as humans. They could see only the material needs of man.

Since that day, even the world has changed its viewpoint. In nurseries where all of the material needs are met; if children do not receive love, they die. It is evident in all of the modern psychological admonitions to parents and institutions that love is an essential element to our growth. Children who are deprived of love in infancy and childhood find it difficult to relate to other people when they grow up.

How often have we who are Christians yielded to that first temptation? We give to the United Fund rather than becoming a part of the personal contact with the needy. We give money to feed the hungry rather than going to take them food. We want to give them food without also giving them the Word of God of which we are stewards. We send money for ministry to jails and prisons rather than going ourselves with the Word of love which alone can set men free. We send chaplains to hospitals rather than taking the love of God in our own flesh to pray for the healing of the sick. Man shall not live by bread alone, but by every word of God.

The second temptation as we follow the order of Luke's gospel is to use the authority and power of the world to establish peace in the world. "The devil took him up and showed him all of the kingdoms of the world in a moment of time, and said to him, 'To you I will give all this authority and their glory; for it has been delivered to me, and I give it to whom I will. If you then, will worship me, it will be yours.' " Lk 4:5-7

Jesus was offered the opportunity to use all of the force of armies and the wisdom of man to bring in the Kingdom of God. This is one of the errors of man-made religions—particularly Islam which is a religion of the sword. It was a temptation to enforce the peace of God so that relationships between man and God, and man and man, would be justice and peace. How often have we tried to legislate morality and failed? We pass laws so that we can live together in peace; but there is no peace in our hearts. The laws are not kept; and the lawbreakers are cast into prison in order to keep the peace. Fear and hatred are born out of the enmity of the people, and there is no peace. The pages of history bear witness to the failure of man to be able to establish justice in the world through the use of external force.

The law had already been tried in Israel, but the people could not keep the law. When the law failed, God sent the prophets; but the people would not hear the prophets. Though they called Israel back to God with the power of the Word of God present in their very midst, the people would not respond. They continued their stiff-necked way. Even when they were bent under the yoke of their captors, they did not repent. The law failed to produce righteousness. The law could not give life; it could only declare that those who did not keep the law deserved death.

How often we act out of the feeling that if we can cause a child enough pain, the child will shape up. The jails are full of those who were abused as children, and who abused their own children. There is no amount of power or pain that can change a person's inside from the outside. The change must come from within.

Jesus did not choose to use the authority that we find in force, whether it be in government or in family. He rejected the authority that lords it over people; and he chose instead to turn the world upside down. He chose to use the authority of love—the authority of service to others. He knew that men would never be able to live together by virtue of pressure from the outside. They had to be changed from within. They had to be made a new creation. I recall the first manifestation of the recent Holy Spirit renewal found many strange bedfellows because the whole of the traditional Church was oppressing those members that were involved in the strange things that were going on. There was unity for a time because of the persecution; but as the pressure began to subside, the inner core that had shown such a unity fell apart because they had not been drawn together by love.

Jesus' response to Satan came out of the knowledge that there would be no union without love. ''Get thee behind me Satan for it is written, 'Thou shalt worship the Lord thy God, and him only shalt thou serve.' '' Lk 4:8 The reality of that worship, and the power of that relationship comes only as we come to know God—as we commit ourselves to walk in the will of the Father.

As the judgments of the world are set aside, and we come to know the love that our Father has for us, we find a new light on the area of good and evil. We find that we can never know true good and evil until we receive that knowledge from God Himself. It is not the wisdom of the world; it is the Holy Spirit who comes to lead us into all truth. Neither the codes of our society nor the rules of the Church are able to know and interpret the life that God has for each of us as we walk in the Spirit.

I remember a father who was led by the Lord to turn his son over to the juvenile authorities because the son did not conform to the rules of the household. Not only was the rest of the family against him, but the whole community tried to point out how he was mistaken in what he was doing. They were quick to judge the man as not loving his son.

When time had passed, it was evident that what the father had done was the turning point in the boy's life. It had made the child aware of the fact that someone cared enough to check him in his life of destruction toward himself. He found a new direction in which to move with his life, and he has become an asset to any community that he might choose to live in. The father had been judged wrong by the community, but he had been shown to be right by God.

That does not mean that every parent who has trouble with a child should turn the child over to juvenile authorities. It means that we are called to listen to the Lord as He gives direction even when it means going against the judgment of the community. It is not the community but God who can interpret the good and evil of each situation as we walk with Him. Jesus made it clear that we are not to throw stumbling blocks in the path of the brethren by judging them at every turn. "Judge not that ye may not be judged. For with the judgment ye judge, ye shall be judged; and with the measure ye mete, it shall be measured to you again." Mt 7:1-2

There was a time when I was condemned by my brethren for some of my beliefs. I was criticized by my clergy brethren in my area because I sought to teach and to live the life of the Holy Spirit. I was condemned by my charismatic brethren because I believed some things contrary to their doctrine. It was not a matter of salvation. It had to do with some of my experience in ministry. I was sure at the time, and I am sure now that the Lord had called me to the ministry, and so I received it and used it. Their condemnation issued from fear. I knew that; but I had a reaction that issued from my pride. I promptly retaliated by condemning them.

It did not make me feel any better. My relationship with the world was no better, and my relationship to me was far worse. I felt that I had to justify myself to them, and I was bound to prove to them that I was right. The Lord spoke to me in that situation to tell me that I had to forgive them. That would not have been so bad; but He also said that I had to ask them to forgive me. I purposely refused to hear that admonition from prayer and from scripture because I did not want to obey.

I wanted to justify myself, and God was quite patient with me. He waited until I could see that I was becoming just like the people I was condemning. At that point I was willing to forgive. I was not able, but I was willing; and God was able. His work began within me to enable me to forgive, and I was willing to ask for forgiveness. I still believe that I am right in my belief. I was wrong in my actions. I had reinforced the separation that was between us. I had not sought the reconciliation with which we are charged as the children of God. Until I was willing to forgive, I was not free.

The use of the law is a subtle thing in our lives. We were reared with the hand of correction from the exterior and generally from the posterior. It is easy for us to fall into the trap of believing people can be changed for the better using that kind of force. We will not find the wisdom to correct that error in the world, but from Jesus, "You have heard that it was said, 'You shall love your neighbor and hate your enemy.' But I say unto you 'Love your enemies and pray for those who persecute you so that you may be sons of your Father who is in heaven.' " Mt 5:43-45

The third temptation is one which gives us another glimpse of the way in which God will work. Satan has a good knowledge of the scripture, and he used that knowledge as he tempted Jesus. He took Jesus and set Him on the highest pinacle of the temple, and said, "If thou be the son of God, cast thyself down from hence; for it is written, 'He shall give his angels charge over thee, to keep thee; and in their hands they shall bear thee up, lest at any time thou dash thy foot against a stone.' "

Jesus answered him out of the scriptures. "It is said, 'Thou shalt not tempt the Lord thy God.' " Lk 4:9-12   In this temptation, we find that we are dealing with initiative. Certainly God will watch over His own. We are admonished to test God—to prove Him. That means that we are to live as He has directed us so that we might know in our own experience that God is faithful. We are NOT to tempt God. We are not to try to get God to do our will in matters where He has not directed us.

Jesus did not go around doing what He thought was good, and then ask the Father to work it out for Him. He did nothing except what He saw the Father doing. The words that He spoke were not His own. They were the words that He was given to speak by the Father. We are called to walk in that same communion that Jesus had with the Father so that we might test God and not tempt Him.

There are times when I would like to roll out a big miracle to impress people with the power of God, but I am sure that it would not help anything. If it would be helpful, then God would get it done. I have often heard people pray, "Lord, if you will only heal so and so, it sure would be a great witness to the people around her." We want God to do something to make people come to faith.

God has elected to draw people to Himself through love. Love is the great miracle. It would not be hard for me to believe that God could put together a miracle. It is hard for me to believe that God loves someone like me. When people respond to the love that God has for them, then miracles follow. There is generally some faith response prior to the miracle either from the person who receives it or from an intercessor. The signs follow the faith; but it is the love that holds people close to the heart of God.

Jesus gave no sign to His generation in the flesh, except the sign of Jonah. "For as Jonah became a sign to the men of Ninevah, so will the Son of man be to this generation." Lk 11:30 The Father had told Jesus to love men into the Kingdom—not dazzle them. A ministry of miracles fades; the love of God is eternal. I have never been bored listening to people talk about the love of God.

Tommy Lewis related one of the best illustrations that I have heard on the subject. If Jesus had decided to jump off the temple, and someone had seen Him, there would have been a larger crowd on the next day for a repeat performance. The crowd would have grown daily for a while; but sooner or later someone would have said to a friend, "Come on let's go over and watch Jesus jump off the top of the temple. He's going to jump in about half an hour."

The friend might have responded, "Naw, He does that every day. Let's go fishing now, and we can catch Him some time next week." Men did not follow Jesus because of the miracles. They may have brought people to have miracles worked for them; but those who followed Him had to walk dusty roads for miles between the miracles. They followed Jesus because in His presence there was a love and peace that they knew in no other place. I have seen many miracles, and I have heard of many others, but the one story that holds my attention is the miracle of God's love for us.

In times that Christians walk through their trials seeking to follow God's will, it feels like it would be a lot easier to cop out. When Jesus hung on the cross, the people stood there mocking Him and spitting on Him. They echoed the voice of Satan, "If you are the Son of God, come down from the cross." Jesus had already found the Father's will in the Garden of Gethsemane. He had prayed, "Father if it be possible, let this cup pass from me, never the less, not my will but thine be done." Lk 22:42 The will of the Father was to remain on the cross, and he would not tempt the Lord His God.

If we seek to walk in the new creation, our dialog with God begins in the garden as we seek His will for our lives. It is not our own wisdom that holds the highest for our lives or the lives of others; it is God's wisdom. There are many who teach about effective prayer as if it is a way to convince God that we are right. They give us techniques to "twist God's arm" so that our will might be done on earth as in heaven. Effective prayer does not begin with technique in speaking to God; it begins with our will to listen to God.

Paul wrote that the whole creation has been subjected to vanity. Our immediate thought might be that it was Satan who did that to us; but it was not Satan, it was God. God subjected the whole creation in hope. God alone held the authority because He was the author of creation. He subjected it by giving oversight to Satan. That is the claim that Jesus heard from Satan and did not dispute in the temptation.

When God created the universe to pass away, He created it in hope that we would choose to live with Him and not pass away with it. That is the only scheme of things that gives us free choice to remain in hell or enter the Kingdom. His love will not allow Him to compel us to come in. He sent His Son to tell us of that love and to show us that love. Jesus came to invite us to enter the Kingdom and enjoy that love eternally with the Father. In Jesus, God opened the way for us to walk out of hell or remain as we are. How else could His love have been manifest and still allow us the freedom to choose?

Paul writes that we are first found in the form of the first Adam—of the earth. We are found in the likeness of the second Adam only as we die and are raised up in a spiritual form. John insists that we must be born again. That which is born of the flesh is flesh, and that which is born of the spirit is spirit. We are never on neutral ground. We are born in hell. We are the inheritors of the kingdom of death by virtue of our father Adam. When we choose God to be our Father by adoption and grace, we are delivered into the Kingdom of His beloved Son.

It is not a matter of being very good so that we might be delivered; it is a matter of our being delivered so that we might become good. Behavior is not the primary issue of the Christian faith; it is a side effect of our being made new in Jesus Christ. The gospel is not "Be good, or be damned!" It is, "Come out of hell and share the Kingdom prepared from the foundation of the world."

The dualism between good and evil as we meet it, is not a battle between God and Satan. The battle is rather within us as we face the decision to remain in a corrupt creation under the authority of Satan or choose that new creation which is in the grace of Jesus Christ. They are both under the dominion of the one God who uses Satan as a pawn; but confines him to the limits that have been set. There is no ground for fear, there is only cause to rejoice that the Way is open for us to move from the world of conflict and law into the world of grace and love. The Way is open for us to move from the world in which we might strive to get our will done into the world wherein God's will is done—upon earth as in heaven.

The Example of Jesus

As WE BEGIN to look for a pattern of life and ministry, we are wise to look unto Jesus the author and finisher of our faith. He is the revelation of God in our flesh; and He is the revelation of what God means when He says, "Man." He is the Word of God that is spoken into our flesh—the first born of many brethren in the new creation. He comes to give us authority to become the children of God; "born, not of blood nor of the will of the flesh nor of the will of man, but of God." Jn 1:13

There are many who try to reduce the life of Jesus to a new set of laws. That can never be done. Jesus was not a stereotype human; He was a particular person. That is one of the great stumbling blocks. Had He been some sort of super being, and we were exactly alike, He would have been easier for us to accept than the son of Mary born in lowly circumstance.

Jesus dealt with people as particular persons. He did not do the same thing for every person He met. He did not heal the eyes of the lame man, He healed his legs. Jesus did not open the leper's ears, He cleansed his flesh. He let Mary sit at His feet, and He taught Martha to serve with a single mind. He met each particular need with particular grace.

The only constant relationship that Jesus had was with the Father. His relationship to men changed because the men themselves changed. His relationship to the Father was constant because the Father is constant. He lived in continuous communion with the Father, and He admonished us to do the same. He spent time alone to maintain His conversation so that He might be aware of the Father's particular will in meeting the individual problems in the people to whom He ministered. He was the interpretation of the law where ever He walked.

Jesus did not please the Father by keeping the law. He kept the law by pleasing the Father. The language of the law is general. It is not interpreted clearly in each situation, and so we need to find a means whereby we might get a clear interpretation. Decisions must be made if we are to act with purpose. There are precepts in the law that insist on cleanliness; but I have found no passage that tells me when to take out the garbage. I must rely on my own common sense, or I might seek God's will in dealing with His time. God is concerned even over taking out the garbage.

Paul writes, "He who loves his neighbor has fulfilled the law. . . . Love does no wrong to a neighbor; therefore love is the fulfilling of the law." Rm 13:8-10   We are able to love as Jesus loved only as we are in communion with God. We are to walk in the Spirit as Jesus showed us from the time of His baptism. It is in the leading of the spirit that we find the direction for love which is the interpretation of the law for the particular circumstance. If we are to follow Jesus, we make our decisions in the light of the Holy Spirit within us. We cannot interpret the law in our own wisdom. As we walk in the Spirit, God interprets the law in us and for us.

Jesus did not live by precept or law. In walking in communion with the Father, He lived within the law and fulfilled the law. He did not transgress the law in any way. He listened as the Father interpreted the law, and He embodied that interpretation of the law in His own life. He did nothing except what He saw the Father doing. "Truly, truly, I say to you, the Son can do nothing of his own accord, but only what he sees the Father doing; for whatever he does, the Son does likewise." Jn 5:19

A good illustration of Jesus' relationship to the Father may be seen in the story of the man born blind in the ninth chapter of John's Gospel. As Jesus and the disciples were walking down the road, the disciples asked, "Jesus, why was this man born blind? Was it because he sinned or because his parents sinned?" That was a good question from the standpoint of Jewish theology.

As Jesus responded, the answer did not come from Jewish theology. It came from God. "Neither this man nor his parents sinned. He was born blind so the works of God might be seen in him. I must work the works of the one who sent me while it is day. The time is coming when no man can work. As long as I am in the world, I am the light of the world." Jn 9:3-5

Some of that answer probably made no sense to the disciples unless they also heard the conversation that went on between Jesus and the Father. Jesus could have answered the disciples by saying "You guys are asking the wrong question as usual." But He turned to ask His Father instead, "Father, what do you want me to do in this situation? Do you want me to heal this man today?"

The Father's answer was particular and concise. "Son, spit on the ground, and make some mud balls. When you have done that, rub them on the man's eyes, and then send him to wash his face in the pool called Siloam."

That must have been what the Father said because that is what Jesus did.

He was absolutely obedient to the Father. He didn't raise any questions about better ways to do the job. He acted in a way that I would call utter foolishness from the standpoint of the world, and He did it because the Father had spoken.

Most of us would have approached the task a bit differently. When we encountered the blind man, we might say, ''The scriptures say that we are to lay our hands on the sick and heal them,'' or ''The scriptures say that we are to anoint the sick with oil so they might be healed.'' Then we would have gone ahead and laid on hands or anointed the man. Jesus stopped to ask the Father.

If we had stopped to ask the Father, and we received the answer that Jesus received; we very likely would have stopped to argue the point with Him. I know that I would have. I dread the day that God tells me to do something like spitting on the ground and making mud balls. I probably will say, ''Father, that looks so nutty, why can't I just lay hands on him and you heal him? What will these people think when I rub mud on his face and then tell him, 'Your face is dirty, go wash at Siloam'?'' In my heart I would be thinking ''If this doesn't work, I'll look like a fool.'' It would be a lot easier to walk away and leave the man sick.

It is not that God cannot do things the way we would do them. He just seems to have a way He prefers to have them done. I was selling a cross to one of my parishioners one day, and she asked me to bless it at the altar. One of her friends was with her, and said that God could bless it right where we were. It came to me to say that He could also bless it at the altar; and when we had taken the time to ask, we took it to the church to bless it. I do not know why God wanted to do it that way, but that was how it went.

Jesus was absolutely obedient even in the face of ridicule. When a problem came up, He took the time to check it out with His Father. When the Father spoke, Jesus moved. It is this pattern in Jesus' life that we are supposed to follow. It is the only way we can live in the world but not of the world. As we make decisions with respect to our Father in heaven, we are set free from bondage to the world. Jesus did not have to react to the world around Him. He rather loved the world and responded to the voice of the Father. He has made this a possibility for us also, ''for through Him we both have access in one Spirit to the Father.'' Eph 2:18

That access to God in prayer is a major part of our deliverance from bondage to the world. We can now learn to pray as Jesus prayed not simply talking to God, but in dialog of speaking and listening. It is in this prayer relationship that we find the ground for our complete freedom from the world as it was manifest in Jesus. He was not bound by the world since He made no decisions in reaction to the world. He did not avoid the evil in the world. He did not withdraw from those who were not acceptable in social or religious circles. He knew the world and what was in it; and He loved the world in spite of what it was. He touched the world with His love when the Father gave Him commandment. He healed the world that He touched. If we are to follow Jesus, we must begin with a seeking to hear the voice of God so that we might walk in the unfolding revelation of His love.

That is a scary way to live. That is why it is so much easier for us to find a set of rules—so easy for us to find someone else to risk making the decision. That is why it is easier for us to avoid those things that might tempt us and withdraw from the people we do not like. Paul warns that it is scary when he writes "Therefore my beloved, as you have always obeyed, so now, not only as in my presence but much more in my absence, work out your own salvation in fear and trembling; for God is at work in you, both to will and to work for his good pleasure." Phil 2:12-13 It makes clear that our walk by faith is not easy, but it is in God's hands, and it is the only way we will grow to maturity as the children of God.

We might try to avoid this task by saying that it was easy for Jesus because He was God, and we cannot do it because we are only men. The truth is that Jesus was fully man as well as fully God. The author of Hebrews says, "He learned obedience through what he suffered." Heb 5:8 He walked in the same trust we are called to walk in as we learn to listen to God; and He was free to move out on what He heard. He did not rationalize what He heard; He acted on it. In the action, He learned obedience through His experience.

Jesus began His ministry when He was baptized by John in the Jordan. His baptism was not someting that John had recommended for Him; it was what the Father told Him to do. If He had listened to the world, He would have baptized John instead of being baptized by John; but Jesus had heard the Father say, "Son, go down to the Jordan and let John baptize you. I have a gift for you there." After the brief argument with John about the matter of who was to baptize whom, Jesus was baptized. Coming up out of the water, the Holy Spirit descended upon Him, and a voice from heaven said, "Thou art my beloved Son in whom I am well pleased." Mk 1:11

The Holy Spirit was poured out on His human flesh so that He could conduct His ministry as a human. He was here to show us what we are to do in the power of the Holy Spirit. God as Holy Spirit is not an option for the Christian; He is a necessity. That was the reason John, the Baptist was so excited about the one who was to come to baptize with the Holy Spirit. The Spirit was both a mark of the end time and the power of enablement for men who were seeking the Kingdom. It was the power of the Spirit that we see in the ministry of Jesus. It was the power of the same Spirit who transformed the fearful disciples into the Apostles who changed the world through the gospel of God in Jesus Christ.

As we pointed out in the last chapter, the Holy Spirit did not surround Jesus in a plastic bubble to keep Him safe from the world. He cast Him out into the wilderness to be tempted by Satan. So often this happens to a person who receives the power of the Holy Spirit into his life. He experiences the newness of life the Spirit brings for awhile, and then all hell breaks loose in his life. That is not to say that God tempts him. "God cannot be tempted with evil and he himself tempts no one." Ja 1:13   It is evident from the scripture though that God, the Holy Spirit does lead us into temptation, even as He led Jesus. We must make our decisions about following God into the new creation as we begin our walk in the Spirit.

When the temptation was complete, Jesus came into Galilee preaching, "The time is fulfilled, the Kingdom of God is at hand; repent ye, and believe the gospel." Mk 1:15   That was the message that He came to bring—the Kingdom of God is at hand. That is the good news. The power is at hand to set men free. God is at hand to save.

When that gospel was preached by Jesus, things happened. Men responded to receive the hope of the Kingdom, and they opened their lives to receive the power of the gospel. Demons responded in fear and trembling. When the gospel was preached, the ministry of healing and casting out demons followed. The ministry was the direct outgrowth of the power in the preaching.

Someone once said the first thing that Jesus did as He met people was to love them. He didn't say the words, "I love you." but His actions spoke the message clearly. Jesus was the very presence of the incarnate love of God revealing these words to the world. He saw no difference between the love of the Father coming into the world and the Kingdom of God being present in their midst. He proclaimed the message with His words and with His actions—even to laying down His life on the cross for those who crucified Him.

As He preached one day in the synagogue in Capernaum, He was confronted by a man who was possessed by an unclean spirit. We are not told how long the spirit had the man; but it is evident that the spirit was stirred up when the gospel was preached. The man shouted (actually the spirit within the man shouted) " 'Let us alone; what have we to do with thee, thou Jesus of Nazareth? Art thou come to destroy us? I know thee who thou art, the Holy One of God.' And Jesus rebuked him saying, 'Hold thy peace and come out of him.' " Mk 1:24-25   The demons knew Him, and when the gospel is preached they tremble. When the power of the gospel is manifest, they flee.

I remember a meeting I attended when I first became aware of the power of the Holy Spirit in the Christian life. Dennis Bennett was speaking. The gospel was being preached, and you could feel the power of God in the place. Suddenly a woman screamed, and her body was convulsed. As I watched, I knew that it was something that she could not do voluntarily. I was rather frightened because it was beyond the realm of my experience and knowledge.

Fortunately there were some there who were not frightened. They had dealt with the problem before. They simply took her out of the room, and delivered her from the demon that assaulted her when stirred by the power of the gospel. She was brought back into the room in her right mind and in the peace of God. The demon had been there for some time, but it had not been a great deal of trouble for the woman. It had been stirred up by the gospel, and cast out by the power of the same gospel.

Jesus followed the exorcism with the healing of Peter's mother-in-law, and the response of the town to the preaching, healing and casting out was immediate. They brought all of the sick and the possessed to Him so that Jesus might free them. That established the pattern for the ministry of Jesus. He would preach the gospel, heal the sick, and cast out demons. The preaching of the Kingdom was the ground for all deliverance whether it be from illness or possession.

The next day, Jesus got up and went out to talk with His Father. His conversation might have gone something like this. "Father, we really had a good meeting last night. A lot of people got saved, and healed and delivered."

"I know, Son, I was there too. Remember?"

"Do you want me to have another service tonight? I think that with the people that were there last night talking about it, we might even have more. Just what do you want now, Father? Remember, I'm new at this."

The Father was not distracted by the response of the people. "Go to the next town and preach, son. Tell them about my Kingdom being at hand. That is what I sent you here to do. We'll take care of the people here in another way."

About that time the disciples came on the scene to take Him back to town. They were excited. They had never been to a healing service before, nor had they ever seen such deliverance from demons. They didn't want to let a good thing get away. "Lord, they are looking all over town for you. Don't you care? Lord, we have a real good thing going now. Why don't we open our own synagogue? We could probably even build a new temple with the kind of services you put on."

Jesus said, "Let us go to the next towns, that I may PREACH there also; for therefore I came forth." Mk 1:38 The order seemed to be important to the Father and so it was to the Son also. The preaching comes first. The preaching of the Kingdom is the source of power for the ministry.

Once when He was in Capernaum, it came to the attention of the people that

He was there, and they came in droves. There were so many of them they could not all get in—those who came late were not even able to get to the door. When they were assembled, He preached to them. While He was preaching, four men came carrying a paralytic on a stretcher. When they could not get him through the crowd, they went up on the roof and tore a hole in it to let the man down in the room where Jesus was. When Jesus saw their faith, He turned and said, "Son, be of good cheer, thy sins be forgiven thee." Mk 2:5

There were some there who took issue with what He said because only God could forgive sins. They were not ignorant of the words of scripture. They knew what scripture said, they just did not know what it meant. Jesus was aware that they had reacted to what He had said; and He used that moment as an opportunity to teach. He wanted to make the point that the Kingdom of God was at hand in power to forgive men their sins. "Why do you question in your hearts? Which is easier, to say to the paralytic, 'Your sins are forgiven,' or to say, 'Rise, take up your pallet and walk?' But that you might know that the Son of Man has authority on earth to forgive sins . . ." Mk 2:8-10

The process within the man would be the same whether it was pronounced in terms of forgiveness or healing. In essence, He is saying, "That part of you which was in bondage is now dead. You have been made new by the power of the Kingdom. That part of you that has been touched by the power of God is a new creation. That is what makes the two statements the same in effect."

Jesus did not condemn people. He did not come to condemn the world, but that the world through Him might be saved. He did point out to some that they were at odds with the Kingdom; but He did not condemn them. John says that they were already condemned and would remain so unless and until they received the one who was in their midst. ". . . he who does not believe is condemned already because he has not believed in the name of the Son of God." Jn 3:18

When Jesus was accused of casting out demons by the authority of Beelzebul, the chief of the devils, He did not condemn those who accused Him. He simply pointed to the fact that those of Israel who cast out demons would be their judges. Men would be judges by the means they used to judge others. If they did not judge, then they would not be judged.

The Jews were zealous for knowledge of the scriptures. They studied them at great length to find the will of God in Torah. I remember being impressed when my Old Testament professor told us of a classmate that he had who could push a pin down through the pages of Torah, and tell you every Hebrew letter through which it passed. They were not ignorant of the scriptures; they were ignorant of God. Being ignorant of God as He is, they created their own God as they would like Him to be. To them Jesus says, "You search the scriptures, because you think that in them you have eternal life; and it is they that bear witness to Me." Jn 5:39   Later in the same passage He talks about who their accuser will be. "Do not think that I shall accuse you to the Father; it is Moses who accuses you, on whom you set your hope." Jn 5:45

That is a hard saying; but it will prove to be true. I have some friends who are so centered in the scriptures that they could not hear God if He spoke to them. If Jesus walked into the room where they were sitting, and said, "I have come for you so that you might live with me," they would grab their Bibles and see if He conformed to their interpretation of scripture. I am convinced that even those who have sought to find truth in the world instead of following the revelation of God in Christ will be judged by the world. We will be judged by our own idols.

The judgment of God does not condemn, it purges. Isaiah was aware of that when he prophesied, "Come let us reason together. Though your sins are like scarlet, they shall be whiter than snow." Isa 1:18 and again as he speaks of the cleansing of Jerusalem, he says, ". . . when the Lord shall have washed away the filth of the daughters of Zion and cleansed the bloodstains of Jerusalem from its midst by a spirit of judgment and by a spirit of burning." Isa 4:4   When we believe that the judgment of God is intended to punish us, we are apt to run from it. It is only as we see it as one aspect of His love that we can seek it until we have been completely purged of our Sin.

The scene of judgment was beautifully illustrated by a vision a young woman shared with me one day. She came to the office terribly upset over the vision, and so I invited her to share it.

She said, "I was standing before the throne of God for judgment. I was the prosecutor, and Jesus was the defense attorney. There were a lot of others there who knew me; and they tried to tell about some of the things that I had done. When they tried to speak, Jesus wouldn't let them."

The situation in the vision witnessed to me as being true. I was at a loss to understand her extreme concern. I thought of the setting in terms of the good news. "Jesus is our defense attorney; and He seeks our acquittal. Why the upset?" I asked.

Her response gave me a glimpse of her self worth, "I was the prosecutor; and I know so much bad about myself. I could never get acquitted."

Her condemnation came from her own self image. This was her idol. It was an idol carved by parents and peers with their "oughts" and "ought nots." She had been thoroughly impressed with her own failure to be and do what she ought to be and do. The answer in the vision seemed so clear. "As soon as you quit prosecuting yourself, you will be acquitted. Jesus will keep the others from condemning you. You are the only one who can keep you from condemning yourself.''

Jesus' concern is not condemnation and punishment. Jesus died that we might not be condemned and punished. His concern is that we die with Him that He might set us free.

To summarize our look at Jesus' life, we find that a pattern is clear. He came to preach the Kingdom; and in the manifestation of its power, He healed the sick and cast out demons. He taught men with authority that they might know and enter into the Kingdom of God which is at hand. He forgave those who were in need of being forgiven when they acknowledged their need in some way, and were willing to receive it on God's terms. He called all men to repentence—to turn from the idols wherein they sought to find meaning and direction for their lives—to know and worship the living God.

Most important, He gave us the pattern of walking in communion with our Father while we are in the world. He called us to learn as little children to walk with God in the family of God. His concern was not that we become preoccupied with our blood lines, but that we see that there is a new family of God—those who hear the Word of God and keep it.

We learn to walk with others who are learning to walk. We learn to talk with others who are learning to talk. We learn to listen with others who are learning to listen. We learn to live as a family because it is as a family that we will live when we come into the fulness of our inheritance. In our learning, we support one another in our weaknesses and we draw from one another's strengths. Together we are being made whole in God's love.

There are times when we act as little children who are playing like we are adults. That is the way we grow up to become adults; but it is also a time when we must learn that we are not yet adults. If we understand this principle, then the adult that we seek to grow and be like will be Jesus. As we grow, we choose the one we seek to follow, and that is why children generally become like their parents. John wrote, ''Beloved, now are we the sons of God, and it doth not yet appear what we shall be; but we know that, when he shall appear, we shall be like him; for we shall see him as he is.'' I Jn 3:2

Deliverance and Authority

As THERE WAS A PATTERN in the ministry of Jesus for setting men free, so there was also a new kind of authority. He rejected the authority of Satan in the temptation; but He did all things with a measure of authority. It is important for us to know the nature of that authority if we are to follow Him. There has been much confusion caused by taking our own images of authority to the scriptures when we try to interpret the life of Jesus.

Jesus taught with authority. He did not teach as the scribes by citing endless genealogies to trace their teaching back to Moses. He taught as directly from God. The Sermon on the Mount gives us an illustration of His teaching in this manner as He cited the common teaching, and then accentuated the teaching with His own statement. "You have heard that it was said to the men of old, 'You shall not kill; and whoever kills shall be liable to judgment.' But I say unto you that everyone who is angry with his brother shall be liable to judgment; whoever insults his brother shall be liable to the council, and whoever says, 'You fool!' shall be liable to the hell of fire." Mt 5:21-22

Jesus taught in a light that brought external action into the light of internal condition. He taught that what man said and did were just symptomatic of his interior state. It was not the outside that mattered so much as the heart within. The heart had to be changed. It has to become pure before we can see God; and it can be made pure only by God's creative love.

If I steal, it is because something within me is amiss. I am fearful that I will lack something that I need; I feel insecure without the things that I lack; I have a compulsion to take things that are not mine; I want to prove my ability to get away with it to prove how smart I am; I dislike myself and I invite punishment in this way are all possible inner states that might lead me to steal something. The inner condition must be healed even as the behavior pattern is changed. If I change the behavior without the inner change of heart, I am still in sin.

"You have heard it said, 'Thou shalt not commit adultery,' but I say unto you, 'He who looks after a woman with lust in his heart already commits adultery.' " Mt 5:27-28   The condition precedes the action. It is good if we stop before the action; but the condition is Sin at its source. The teaching of Jesus carried with it the authority to heal the interior and cast out any spirit that moves us to compulsive action.

Jesus' concern in teaching was to enable people to open their hearts to the Spirit who works the internal changes in us. He sought to turn their eyes from the sinful action to the sinful condition. He sought to bring them from self justification to confession of Sin. He was concerned that the people see the possibility of knowing God as He knew the Father—that in Father's love, hearts might be made new.

Jesus taught them about the Kingdom so that they might enter into relationship with God as King. He sought to undo the error that Israel and Judah made when they chose to have their own king and set God aside from being King over them. Jesus taught as one who knew the reality. "The Kingdom of God is at hand." "The Kingdom of God is like . . ." His actions were in accord with His words. His authority was grounded in the integrity of His life in union with the Father. He taught men that the law was not to pass away. It was to be interpreted by the Spirit in any given situation. In every place and at any time, God's will for us is specific. When I come to know Him through the Holy Spirit, I find that His will for me is an interpretation of the law for that time and place.

The authority of Jesus is seen today in teaching when a person is able to hear the gospel through a teacher. Frequently we will hear people witness to grasping the revelation of God as a servant of God speaks. I have seen people who have been Christians most of their lives have their ears opened to the gospel for the first time when they hear someone teach with authority. There is an authority that I have because of my position; but that does not enable me to communicate the gospel. That is an external authority which can only give me opportunity to speak. The authority of Jesus is an authority that enables me to communicate.

My own experience in seminary was frustrating because I had to write papers about what other men thought and said. I could quote Barth and Bultmann; but I was never told that I must decide what I believed and what I would say. It is only as we leave the quotations of others and begin to speak from our own faith and our own experience that we leave the teaching of the scribes and enter the realm of the authority of Christ.

I once had to cope with a case in which one of my friends had asked a Baptist friend to be God parent for a baby. My concern was twofold. I was concerned that the friend be a baptized believer in Jesus. I was also concerned that she be able to take the vows as the God parent of an infant in good conscience. I was aware of the Baptist doctrine of Baptism; and so I decided to go to the girl and ask her.

We talked a bit about the friendship and the new baby, and then I began the questioning. "Are you baptized?"

"Yes."

"Can you take the vows that you will be asked to take as a God parent? Do you believe this child will be regenerated by the power of the Holy Spirit? In other words, are you willing to accept infant baptism?"

She thought a bit, and finally replied, "I'd better go talk to my pastor to find out what I believe." She had placed her faith in her pastor. She was living in a spiritual wilderness because she had not known the authority of Jesus to set her free to ask God for herself. She did not know that the Kingdom was still at hand.

When we lay hold of the authority of Christ to teach, we are apt to become convinced that we have all of the answers. The truth is that He has all the answers. We are simply used as channels to communicate them. There are times when we will be in the will of Jesus, and times when we will be out of it. The Holy Spirit is the source of our authority. When we are out of the Spirit, we must trust Him to protect those we are teaching from confusing our words with the absolute truth.

I know that Jesus teaches through me. I have given my ministry to Him and He has given me the gift of Himself. The Holy Spirit speaks Jesus through me. I also know that I am an earthen vessel. My words are not always adequate to express God's truth. The images I use are not full enough to communicate Jesus Christ. I know that some of my pet beliefs are hard to relinquish. I speak God's Word, but I also include my error.

We only have one teacher, but He uses a multitude of voices to speak to us. He has to use a multitude because there is not one that is perfect other than His own. We need to ask God to enable us to hear His voice whenever He speaks and through whom He speaks. Since He uses sinners—that's all He has to use—we will hear both God and man—both Spirit and flesh. If we are unaware of that fact, we might well confuse the flesh with the Spirit and follow where we are not led of the Lord.

I once heard a woman quote me from one of my tapes, and it scared me to find that she took every word that I had spoken as gospel. I have learned to pray before I talk, that the Holy Spirit will cover the gap between flesh and Spirit that the people of God might not be led astray. "Father, I ask that you grant me the grace of your Holy Spirit. Take my mind and my heart, and think with them. Take my lips and my tongue, and speak with them; that my thoughts might be your thoughts and my words your words. Grant to your people ears to hear and hearts to understand, and the wisdom to discern between my error and thy truth; that in the sharing of your Holy Word, we might all be brought to a greater knowledge and love and service of thee. In Jesus Christ, our Lord.''

Jesus cast out demons with authority. He did not use the incantations and props of the regular Jewish exorcists. He ordered the demons with a word of power, and the demons fled. ''He commands them with a word and they obey.'' Mk 1:27   This was a new teaching. The Jews had seen nothing like it before. The power to command demons was not to be found among men.

David had cast out demons through singing psalms to the sound of his harp, but they would later return. From the Apocryphal Book of Tobit, we read of Tobit driving Asmodeus out of the marriage chamber by burning bits of fish liver and heart. The reason the demon did not come back was that the archangel Raphael pursued him to northern Egypt and bound him with chains. Solomon was reputed by the historian Josephus to be so wise that he would write incantations to cast out demons so that they would never return.

Jesus simply ordered them out with a word. The old means of exorcism has been set aside and a new power has been manifest. The early Christian Church followed Jesus in the use of the word of authority which is the Name of Jesus. The Christian exorcists did not operate as did others. There were some exorcists who were not of the faithful who apparently were successful in using the power of the Name of Jesus. Luke records, ''Master, we saw a man casting out demons in your name, and we forbade him, because he does not follow with us.'' But Jesus said to him, ''Do not forbid him; for he that is not against you is for you.'' Lk 9:49-50

All of those who tried to use the name of Jesus without also being a follower did not fare so well. The sons of Sceva are notable examples of some who tried to use the power and authority of Jesus without the power of the Holy Spirit. The seven went in to cast a demon out of a man, and said, ''I adjure you by the Jesus whom Paul preaches.'' The evil spirit answered them saying, ''Jesus I know, and Paul I know, but who are you?'' Where upon the possessed man leaped up and attacked them, and drove them out of the house naked and wounded. Acts 19:13ff

How different was Paul's experience with the slave girl in Philippi who had the spirit of divination. She followed Paul for many days saying, ''These men are servants of the Most High God who proclaim to you the way of salvation.'' Paul finally got annoyed, and turned and said to the spirit, ''I charge you in the name of Jesus Christ to come out of her.'' And it came out that very hour. Acts 16:16ff   I think it notable that Paul did not go around casting out demons just because they were there. It almost seems that he waited until he got all of the advertising that he needed before he got rid of the spirit that was broadcasting.

I had someone come into the office one afternoon who seemed to me as if she needed exorcism. I asked her a few questions that would give me some insight into the matter, and she became very fearful. When I asked what she was afraid of, she responded with a descripton that someone had given her of an exorcism. She had to lie on a table while people put all manner of strange things on her and did their incantations over her. Having never had such an experience, I did not blame her for being fearful. It would have scared me to have to go through what she described. It was an eye-opening description for me that pointed out the difference between the old mode of exorcism and the word of power which is able to set people free without fear of return.

Jesus had the authority to forgive sins. The encounter with the paralytic on the stretcher brought that out clearly. He was able with a word to remove all barriers that stood between man and God. The power of Jesus to forgive is not just the power to excuse them for what they have done. It is not simply taking away their guilt. It is both of these and more. It is the regeneration of their very being so that they might stand justified before God. By the power of His forgiveness, He sets us into a new relationship with our Father.

The same authority was committed to the disciples when He breathed on them, and said, ''Receive the Holy Spirit. If you forgive the sins of any, they are forgiven; if you retain the sins of any, they are retained.'' Jn 20:22   This is one of the primary authorities committed to the Church by Jesus; and it stands in the midst of a missionary charge. When we read the rest of John's Gospel, we realize that forgiveness may come through bringing the light of Christ into the darkness of man in any way, as well as saying with power, ''I forgive you.''

John's concept of forgiveness is our being set free to abide in Christ and having Christ abide in us. Forgiveness is that positive power of creation that enables us to become what God has called us to be. When we exercise the authority to forgive as Jesus has given it to us, we often see that power manifest in the flesh of the one set free.

I had a woman in one of my parishes that was sick with a continual bleeding. She sought the Lord to find out what she was to do. She was told to make her confession. I was her confessor, and I was out of town; so she argued with God to put it off. He would have no part of that; so she finally made contact with the priest who was supplying for me while I was on vacation. He was glad to meet with her to witness her confession and to pronounce God's absolution with the authority that Jesus gave us. When the woman walked out of the church that day, she was healed. The cause of the sickness and the sickness itself had been removed.

I have heard many confessions in my life as a priest; and I have yet to find a person who did not know that something happened to set them free in the process. The great problem that we have is accepting the fact that we are to confess our sins one to another and forgive one another. When we wield the authority to forgive, we set people free. Counselling has been set in place of confession by many today; but it is not the same thing. I have had people come into the office and pour out all of the lurid details of their lives in a counselling situation. When they do, I always suggest that we take the time to go to the chapel and tell it to God. They usually feel that they have already confessed to God, but many of them try it because I have suggested it so strongly. Thus far all of them find an appreciable difference when they have made their confession to God and have heard His absolution pronounced in the authority of Jesus.

Jesus had authority over the elements of nature. When He was in the boat in the midst of the storm on the Sea of Galilee, He commanded the storm to be still and it was quiet. He walked on the waters of that sea in the chaos of a storm; and He even gave Peter the authority to walk with Him. He was able to ride through a screaming throng of people on an unbroken colt of a donkey. He had authority over the things of the old creation.

Jesus never showed any authority OVER men. He called some to follow Him. Some of them did. Certainly the twelve responded to the call. All of them did not. The rich young man walked away very sad because he could not accept the call on Jesus' terms. Jesus loved Him very much, but the love that He had for the man would not let Him impose His will. Jesus made no bones about the condition of the Pharisees in their self righteousness, but He did not argue with them to convince them that He was right and they were wrong. He offered to every man the love of the Father and the freedom that love can bring. He offered it through preaching, teaching, healing, casting out demons, and forgiving; but He allowed each person the choice to receive that love or reject it.

The whole basis for Jesus' authority was to be found in love. That love issued in service to those who were willing to receive what He offered. Furthermore, He gave us a commandment to do the same. "A new commandment I give unto you, that you love one another as I have loved you." Jn 13:35 He did not give us authority OVER one another. He gave us authority to support one another. It is a kind of authority UNDER one another—the power to meet each other's needs in the Body of Christ.

James and John were walking the road with Him one day. The other ten were apparently not within ear shot; so they took advantage of the situation to ask Jesus for a favor. Jesus was always open to those who asked, "What can I do for you?"

"We would like to sit one on your right hand and the other on your left when you come into your Kingdom." They saw the Kingdom of God as being just a higher reflection of the kingdoms of earth. They were really asking for the honor of sitting next to Jesus so they would be able to bask in His glory.

Jesus did not reprimand them. He very patiently asked them to consider what they were asking, and if they were ready to do all that they must do to sit in the Kingdom at all. By the time the discussion had reached its end, the other ten had become aware that something was going on. When they found out what James and John were up to, they were angry with them. They wanted a crack at those seats too.

Jesus finally decided to settle the issue for them. He called them together to clarify the nature of authority in the Kingdom of God. "You know that those who are supposed to rule over the Gentiles lord it over them, and their great men exercise authority over them. But it shall not be so among you; but whoever would be great among you must be your servant, and whoever would be first among you must be slave of all. For the Son of Man also came not to be served but to serve, and to give his life as a ransom for many." Mk 10:42-25   In short Jesus has taken the way in which we normally perceive authority, and He has turned it upside down.

There are still some who insist that they have authority over others in the name of Jesus. There are some who insist that the others must let them be the servants in the name of Jesus. There is not a great deal of difference in my imposing my will on you in an overbearing manner or a servile manner. It is the imposition of the will that love forbids. Imposition is of the authority of the world.

I must see that my calling is first to know God. Until I do know Him, I cannot wield the authority that He gives to man. As I come to know Him and to know His will for me, I can then offer to each person that I meet the gift that God has given to me for him. I must first receive from God. I must then know His will in the distribution of what he has given. Then I must give to each person as God directs.

I once heard the Provost of Coventry Cathedral say, "When we are asked to take on any task, we must first ask what instruments of authority we will have to wield. If we are not willing to use that which is given, then we must leave the task alone." If we are not willing to receive and wield the authority of Jesus, then we might well leave the gospel alone. The Kingdom of God cannot be brought in by the authority of the world.

Jesus said it in a little different way. "For which one of you desiring to build a tower, does not first sit down and count the cost, whether he has enough to complete it? Otherwise, when he has laid the foundation, and is not able to finish, all who see it begin to mock him, saying, 'This man began to build, and was not able to finish.'" Lk 14:28-29   The cost that we must pay to wield the authority of God is to relinquish the control of the results.

For me to wield the authority of Christ means that I must be concerned to do the will of God as I perceive it, and not be worried about the results. I must seek more than anything else to determine the will of God for me and do it. It is a matter of learning to listen for His voice—to be led by the Spirit. I am to practice listening and obeying, and letting God be responsible for the results.

That does not leave me free to cop out. It does not mean that I can do as I please and blame the results on God. It rests on my own intention to come to know God—and listen to Him. It rests on my commitment to do, as nearly as I am able, what God wants me to do so that He can accomplish in me and through me what He wants done. It is what we call an obedience orientation toward God in which we must be totally dependent on Him to forgive our errors and turn them to His glory while we learn to walk in closer obedience in the Kingdom.

When I seek to be result oriented, I tend to exercise my Original Sin. I determine what ought to happen, and I do whatever I think will bring it to pass. I plan, and then I ask God to make the plan work, instead of letting God work His plan through me. I become concerned over my own will being done whether God agrees or not. The Church often operates from this viewpoint. We hold our planning sessions with great discussion and much talk. We might even open with a prayer, but we give little time to silence where God might speak to us. We set our goals, and then we ask God to prosper us.

When I pray in a result orientation, I tend to try to get God to do my will. I shift my attention from God to the situation to see if things are going right. Like a golfer who swings a club and takes his eye off the ball, I miss the mark. When things do not go my way, I become anxious, and I count manipulation of people as part of the game. I use the world's authority because I am not able to wield that authority of Jesus which leaves the results in the hands of the Father.

Jesus was always obedience oriented. He knew that the Father had something better mind than man would ever plan. He was not concerned with what happened as a result of His ministry. He was concerned that the Father's will be done. Had he been result conscious—seeking what He wanted, He would likely have worked out a way to avoid the cross. His authority rested squarely on His willingness to be out of control with complete trust in the Father. This would have been impossible for Him had He not known the Father, and been in communication with Him.

The Church often fails to wield the authority of Jesus because she is not willing to be obedience oriented. She is not willing to be out of control because she does not know the One who is in control. When the Church fails to trust God to do His will through her, she fails to pay the cost of building her tower, and the building is not completed. How different it is when the Church first seeks to know the Father—when it follows the teaching of Jesus to seek first His Kingdom and His righteousness and begins to move in His will.

I know that in my own experience, I have a tendency to be result oriented. If things do not turn out the way I think they should, I tend to get upset. I try to second guess God. With the upset comes the anxiety and guilt—the feeling that I didn't do something right. If I had just done it right, it would have worked. I should have been able to do something to make it work. It means that I have taken things in my own hands, and I want to be God. If I can get away from things when that begins to happen, I can turn it all back over to God. When I see it to be His problem to work out, I can once again find that peace that He gives; and I can move in His will.

I keep forgetting that the appearance of the cross in the life and ministry of Jesus must have been a proclamation of failure to all of those around Him. The disciples certainly seemed to have taken it that way. Yet contrary to the judgment of men, it was the proclamation of victory that paved the way for the new creation of God. As long as we keep judging God's actions, we will be hesitant to exercise the authority of Christ. We will be hesitant to give up the control of results in our lives.

When we do not trust God to do His will, we will wind up relying on our own power. The Church has received the call from God to set men free in His power. When she fails, it is generally because she is trying to do God's work with man's power. She then begins to rationalize the failure of God instead of turning to Him for the resolution of the power problem. At that point, the Church has placed herself directly between the world and God.

I frequently used to find myself defending God against the world. I could never win because I was always on the world's turf. When we argue, we begin to use our knowledge and our wisdom. We use the world's methods. I found that it was far better to let God handle the arguments. I invite those in the world who would like to argue to try God in their own lives—to take any situation they like, and ask God to reveal Himself there. It stops a lot of arguments, and it has led a number of people to meet God.

When we fail to show the power and authority of God to set men free, we often pick up the authority and power of the world, and we call it the authority of God. The tragedy is not simply that we are not bringing God's power to bear on the problems of man; but we don't do as well with the world's methods as the world does. Our foundation to our tower might be laid, but the walls are not up; and yet we stand strutting like peacocks believing that our building is complete. We are offering Jesus Christ to the world for less than He is because we are not aware of all that He is.

We must also consider the meaning of authority as it appears in John's prologue to his Gospel. "He came to his own home, and his own people received him not. But to all who received him, who believed in his name, he gave power (authority) to become children of God; who were born, not of blood nor of the will of the flesh nor the will of man, but of God." Jn 1:11-13 Jesus gives us authority to become new beings. As the author of creation, He rewrites us into new creatures.

When we examine the word for authority that John uses, we find that it is composed of two words. It is the Greek exousia. We are all familiar with the meaning of "ex." It means "out of." We see a form of it used in public buildings marking the way out. The second word is "ousia" which means substance. The early Church fathers used a form of the word when they talked about God, Father, Son and Holy Spirit being homo ousia—of the same substance. It has to do with what we are—with our being. The way the words are linked together tell us something of what the word meant as it was constructed. It meant that we have the authority to DO what we ARE.

Authority in this sense is not legislative. We cannot pass a law that can make us a child of God. We must be changed at the core of our being. The modern Church has become so preoccupied with behavior that we often miss the fact that our being precedes our behavior. To change our behavior in a meaningful way, we must change our being.

Before we can act like children of God, we must be changed into children of God. That takes the authority of Christ. The means of the transformation is our new birth, "Ye must be born again . . . that which is born of the flesh is flesh and that which is born of the spirit is spirit." Jn 3:6 When I am in the flesh, I have authority to act out of the flesh; when I am born of the Spirit, I can then act out of the spirit.

Jesus taught the same thing when He spoke about false prophets being known by their fruits. "Are grapes gathered from thorns, or figs from thistles? So, every sound tree cannot bear evil fruit, nor can a bad tree bear good fruit." Mt 7:16-18

We can wield the authority of God as we become the children of God. Our very substance must be changed, not just our mind. When our substance is changed by the authority of Christ—when we receive Him—then we can bring forth different fruit—exousia—out of our substance.

The new relationship to God gives access to the throne of grace. We can be instruments of God—used for the reconciliation of the world. We no longer seek to make men conform to a behavior pattern that is acceptable to other Christians. We rather seek to set them free to find the behavior that God has in mind for them. We are to love them, God must do the changing.

The Pharisees were models of morality in their behavior, but they were in the kingdom of their own righteousness—not God's. It was a matter of their making themselves conform to the outward appearance. Whenever we are tempted to make demands on people to conform to particular behavior, we must also offer them the power of God to be changed. We must be able to exercise the authority of Christ who is able to change their BEING, and in so doing, change their behavior.

It is when I am willing to love the people around me that I am also able to see that they will come out into that love to find healing. They will not come out into criticism and condemnation. They will not come out into an environment where someone requires more of them than they are able to give. They will hide and try to cover their Sin, and that is the reason for a great deal of the unforgiven Sin in the people of God in the Church.

Jesus did not have any minimum standards for those He loved. He loved saint and sinner alike. He associated with saint and sinner alike. He healed them when they were open to receive. He set them free from bondage when they were willing to accept freedom, and He loved them with an unconditional love. That was the nature of His authority in His relationship with people.

So often the Christian community will accept those who come in from the world without a great deal of judgment; but once they are in, we require a minimum standard of behavior. We have an expectation that binds them so they cannot continue to grow with any measure of freedom.

I had a woman walk into my office one day who had driven some fifty miles to see me. When she sat down, she asked, "Can you help me?"

I am always a little hesitant to say yes until I know what I am saying, and so I asked, "What's your problem?"

Her story was one that is all too familiar. "I am a member of a prayer group; but when I asked them to minister to me in the problems I have, they say, 'You are a Christian, you should be able to do that yourself.' They just will not help me. Will you help me, please?"

There was only one answer to that question, "Of course!" I also added a bit of advice that I have come to find helpful to me when people try to lock me in a box by telling me what I OUGHT to be able to do for myself as a Christian. "Next time tell them you are not a Christian. They are probably very willing to minister to pagans."

I learned that lesson the hard way. I went to one of the leaders of the Church one day for exorcism. I was told that if I were Spirit-filled, I could do that myself. I was torn between keeping the spirit that was bothering me, and admitting that I was not Spirit-filled. Furthermore, the admission had to be to someone who I wanted to believe that I was Spirit-filled. There was only one way out. I went back to the person, and said, "I am not Spirit-filled then." I did not receive the ministry that I needed from that person; but I received a great deal more in the insight that had set me free from having to meet someone else's minimum standard for Christians.

I heard someone say the other day that the Christians are the only army that kills its wounded. When someone is having trouble laying hold of life, we dump all of their Sins back on them. We do not remit Sin, we reinforce it. It is something like the chicken syndrome. When a chicken is hurt, the others will gather around and peck it to death. When they get started, even the hurt chicken will join the rest—picking at himself.

Jesus exercised an unconditional love toward people. It did not matter how bad they were hurt or how wicked they were. It is this love that we see at the table of Simon when the woman came in to wash His feet with her tears and wipe them with her hair. Simon knew what kind of woman she was, and Jesus also knew. It was in this context that Jesus could talk to Simon in a way he could understand. "A certain creditor had two debtors; one owed five hundred denarii, and the other fifty. When they could not pay, he forgave them both. Now which of them will love him more?"

"Simon answered, 'The one I suppose, to whom he forgave more.'

"Then turning toward the woman he said to Simon, 'Do you see this woman? I entered your house, you gave me no water for my feet, but she has wet my feet with her tears and wiped them with her hair. You gave me no kiss, but from the time I came in she has not ceased to kiss my feet. You did not anoint my head with oil, but she has anointed my feet with ointment. Therefore I tell you that her sins which are many are forgiven, for she loved much; but he who is forgiven little loves little.' And He said to her, 'Your sins are forgiven . . . Your faith has saved you; go in peace.' " Lk 7:40-50

Our ministry must be like that of Jesus if we are to wield the authority He has given us. Mother Teresa, the saint of India who was awarded the Nobel Prize for 1980, carries that love of Jesus into the streets of Calcutta. She lives the gospel that she teaches. She is the incarnation of the love that we see in Jesus. She wields the authority of God because she was willing to pay the price after she had counted the cost. There is no question about her being of God in the minds of the people of India. She is a holy person—a manifestation of the sons of God for which the world is waiting. She loves the unlovable, and she loves them unconditionally; and that is the authority of Jesus.

Jesus said, "He who believes in me will do the works that I do; and greater works than these shall he do because I go to the Father." Jn 14:12 Our ministry finds both its pattern and authority in Jesus. The great commission begins, "All authority is given unto me in heaven and in earth. Go ye therefore . . ." Mt 28:18-19

The authority has been given to Him by the Father—the author of all things; and is now available to us through the indwelling power of the Spirit. We must be aware of that reality for it is the very basis for the existence of the Body of Christ. There is much talk today in major denominations about accepting some forms of immorality that have been rejected by God in scripture. We speak of accepting them because we are not able to wield the authority of Jesus to set free those that are bound by them.

The Church will always have a measure of Sin because we are still in the flesh as well as the Spirit. We are called to confess that Sin and remit it by the power of God. When we fail to exercise that power, and we turn to the world's wisdom to explain our failure, we are guilty of harlotry. When we accept a sinful condition as the will of God, we enter into apostasy such as was seen in the Corinthian that Paul cut off from the Church. We delude the people of God with a lie.

There is no question about the clarity of the gospel that calls all men to be regenerate—to become that new creation which is the Kingdom of God. We are called to die to our old interests and motives, and allow God to fill us with His. We are to reckon ourselves to be dead indeed unto Sin, but alive unto God through Jesus Christ our Lord. That change cannot be made with the authority of the world, or by any effort on our part. It is the gift of God who has begun His work in those who have come to Him for life.

Sanctification
Being Set Free

I AM ALWAYS DELIGHTED when someone walks into the office to share a new commitment to Jesus. If they are new Christians, they are apt to bubble something like, "Father Al, I just wanted to share with you; I gave my life to Jesus; and now I am really a Christian." They usually exhibit the joy of Jesus with them. Some people see them as obnoxious; but I find them a source of joy for me.

What they do not know is that the pilgrimage is not over—it has just begun. The feeling that results from giving as much of ourself as we can to as much of God as we know is usually a dramatic change. God receives the gifts that we offer Him. When we offer Him ourself, He receives us. He begins His work within us to cleanse and recreate our hearts—the memory banks of life.

There was a time in my life as an Episcopalian that I thought altar calls were so much emotional nonsense. I have come to believe differently. I have come to believe, not so much from scriptural proofs as I have from the observation of changed lives. I have seen the difference made in those who have come forward to make the commitment of their lives to Jesus. It is not always a predictable change, but it is a change for the better.

On the other hand, I have never seen anyone who was completely changed at that point. Everyone has to make further commitments as they grow. Jesus said, "If anyone would come after me, let him deny himself and take up his cross daily and follow me." Lk 9:23   Conversion is not a once-in-a-lifetime decision. It is a habitual offering of one's self to God so His continuing work might come to perfection in us.

The people who come in one week with a witness to conversion may well be back the next week wondering where their feeling went. They had expected it to last eternally. Most of them are concerned that they have done something wrong, and God left as suddenly as He had come. I used to warn new Christians about the down-hill slide from the mountain top; but I have come to see no need in rushing into the next step. I have decided that I would do well to enjoy their mountain top with them as long as they are there. I know I will be walking the valley with them soon enough.

God has completed His work FOR us; but He has not completed His work IN us. We are still part flesh and part spirit. That part of us which is not yet renewed is still subject to the devil. It is the source of much of our disease as Satan gets in his licks. That part that is renewed is not subject to Satan. It is free to walk in the Spirit of God. That part of us grows as the flesh continues to die. "Though our outer nature is wasting away, our inner nature is being renewed every day." II Cor 4:16

The Spirit dominates my life when I say yes to God. The patterns of behavior that emerge are God's righteousness. That is not to say that I do nothing wrong in the eyes of men. It is to say rather that what I do is redeemed. It is brought into the realm of God's Kingdom where all things, purified by the fire of God's love, are in God's will.

The flesh, on the other hand, rules my behavior when I am out of the Spirit. Some of the things I do may not be wrong in the eyes of men, but they stand unredeemed by God until I bring them to Him in the Spirit. Whatever righteousness I perceive is self-righteousness. In this event Satan has dominion in my life.

My life style usually vacillates between the two. The way I walk is a matter of decision. If I decide that I want to walk in the Spirit, I do. I may not always be aware of how God is working in my life; but I am assured that He is working. If I invite Him to come in; He will come in. If I forget, and go my way without inviting Him in; He lets me try it my way. The decision is mine; He has already made His. Not to decide is to decide.

Since I am still part flesh, I am open to being indwelt by spirits other than the Holy Spirit—at least in the fleshly part. Since I am partly in the Spirit, I cannot be possessed completely as one who has none of the Spirit. The demonic has access to my flesh; but not to that part of me indwelt by the Holy Spirit.

There has been great debate about Christians and demons. There are some who argue that demons cannot remain within Christians. The issue will never be settled by theological debate. Those who have experienced freedom in their lives through exorcism, have settled the issue as far as they are concerned. Those who have not had such an experience can still believe as they choose.

My initial encounter with the ministry of casting out demons was not with pagans, but with Christians. Most were "born again" and some were "Spirit filled." It did not occur to me to work it out philosophically before we tried it. We decided that we might as well go ahead and try it. Jesus sent us to preach the gospel, and these people had heard it. In their response, they were trying to get the freedom that was promised.

Our experimentation with the power in the Name of Jesus, was a new experience. Christians who were in bondage to fear were set free from fear. Anger was relieved. Anxiety was quenched. Tension was broken. One lady who came to the parish for ministry had suffered from narcolepsy from the time of her last pregnancy. In our discussion of the pregnancy, we found that she had been very angry about her pregnancy. We decided we would try to exorcise a spirit of anger to see what would happen. We had nothing to lose except the spirit, if it happened to be there. The exorcism was successful, and the lady was healed of her narcolepsy.

Part of our difficulty in thinking about our condition as both flesh and spirit— as both saved and unsaved—is our feeling that if God has really done it, then it's done. I always get a little uneasy when I hear people talking about the condition of man in absolute terms. I cannot imagine anyone who has made even a tenative commitment to Jesus being completely out of the Kingdom. I suspect when some of the presumptuous brethren consign some of the nominal brethren to hell, it is their own judgment and not God's.

I do not commend nominal commitment. I agree with Sam Shoemaker who said that we could have a little christianity and feel miserable; or we could have a lot more and feel great. I commend as great a commitment as anyone can muster. We must make the basis of that commitment a choice for entering the Kingdom of God, and not simply staying out of hell. Only then will we tend to give God the maximum instead of the minimum. I have never known anyone who has been completely transformed in this life. If they had been, I am sure that, like Enoch, they would have walked on into the Kingdom of God without having to die.

All of us still have a measure of carnality. It is the flesh in us that causes us to separate from one another. It is the flesh that makes us so quick to judge one another. We try so hard to be mature. In our effort to prove how mature we have become, we demonstrate our immaturity.

When I began to fellowship with the early charismatics, I met all manner of people who were critical of the institutional church. They claimed the church was feeding them milk and not meat they felt they needed to grow. They separated themselves in order to get their meat, and in so doing revealed their carnality. "But I, brethren, could not address you as spiritual men, but as MEN of flesh as BABES in Christ. I fed you with milk, not solid food; for you were not ready for it; and even now you are not ready. For while there is jealousy and strife among you, are you not of the flesh, and behaving like ordinary men?" I Cor 3:1-3

On the other hand, these are the same people Paul had addressed as saints when he opened the epistle. They are the same people he acknowledged to fall behind in no gift as they waited for the Day of the Lord. They were both saint and sinner. They had chosen to follow Jesus; but there were not willing to admit that they might be wrong in any way. They did not yet see that "we know in part and we prophesy in part." They sought righteousness without love and they wound up in separation.

When we make our first decision to follow Jesus as Savior and Lord, we can offer Him only that part of us at the conscious level of our heart and mind. We cannot give Him something we do not have. We may feel that we have ourself in hand, but most of us lies in the unconscious realm. It is hidden from us. It is there because we chose at some level to hide it from ourselves because it is too painful at the conscious level. Our unconscious is out of the control of our will.

Our unconscious holds what scripture calls the secrets of the heart. The psalmist writes of our problem when he says, "Who can understand his errors? Cleanse me from my secret faults." Ps 19:12 He knew he was not in control of his whole life. There were areas of his heart that he did not know about with his mind. He was compelled to trust God in the matter, and so he prays, "Create in me a clean heart, O God, and renew a right spirit in me." Ps 51:10 The problem is that the heart is not yet pure as it must be for us to see God.

Paul speaks of the problem of judging others when we cannot see the content of the heart. ". . . Judge nothing before the time, until the Lord come, who will bring to light the hidden things of darkness, and will make manifest the counsels of the heart, and then shall every man have praise of God." I Cor 4:5 Jesus was clear in his own teaching about the content of the heart. "What comes out of a man is what defiles a man. For from within, out of the heart of man, come evil thoughts, fornication, theft, murder, adultery, coveting, wickedness, deceit, licentiousness, envy, slander, pride, foolishness. All these things come from within, and they defile a man." Mt 7:20-23

Sin is stored in the heart. If we are boastful about our Sin it is at the conscious level. It may also come to the conscious level for the purpose of confession. If we are ashamed, we hide it—even from ourselves—at the unconscious level. It is the heart that needs purification. Only as that healing takes place can we see God. "We see now in a mirror dimly, but then face to face. Now I know in part; then I shall understand fully, even as I have been fully understood." I Cor 13:12

Salvation is not just a matter of getting out of the body and flying up to heaven. Salvation literally means wholeness. As Christians our salvation is that state of perfection that God has prepared for us in Jesus Christ. We are called to nothing less than ''to know the love of Christ which surpasses knowledge . . . and be filled with all the fulness of God.'' Eph 3:19

Our salvation means that the old man is completely dead and buried with Christ. The new man has been completely raised up and perfected in Him. That is a bit different from the normal image of going to some place called heaven; but it is the core of an essential relationship in the Kingdom of God. Without our perfection—our full preparation to live with God in His glory—the heaven we seek might well be an eternal hell for us. ''Our salvation means that we have been tried by fire and shaken out, in order that what cannot be shaken may remain.'' Heb 12:27

Jesus taught that we must lose our life for His sake in order to keep it eternally. Death to self is essential to life with God. Death in the old creation is necessary for us to live in the new. Paul writes about the process of deliverance in Romans 5-8. He lays the foundation in chapter 5. ''God showed His love for us in that while we were still sinners Christ died for us. Since, therefore, we are now justified by His blood, much more shall we be saved by Him from the wrath of God. For if while we were enemies we were reconciled to God by the death of His Son, much more, now that we are reconciled, shall we be saved by His life.'' Rm 5:8-10   It is not in our repression of behavior that we are saved, but by God's direct creative action.

Our salvation requires that we quit striving to ''do it ourself'' and allow God to work with His power. It lies in our death and resurrection. ''As many as are baptized into Christ Jesus were baptized into His death. We were buried therefore with Him by baptism into death, so that as Christ was raised from the dead by the glory of the Father, we too might walk in NEWNESS of life.'' Rm 6:3-4   It is as we die that we are set free from bondage to Sin. As we die the old man passes into oblivion, and Sin has no handhold by which to grasp us.

We are not to seek to avoid death. For us to avoid death is to avoid salvation. We will not slip past the pay window of our Sin. The wages of Sin is death, and we will collect all that we have coming to us. We may stop there or we may go on to the gift window. We have no choice about our wages; we do have a choice to make about the gift. If we choose to go on, ''the gift of God is eternal life in Christ Jesus, our Lord.'' Rm 6:23   The gospel does not claim that we will not die. It proclaims that death has no more dominion over us. We will not die eternally.

When we have been baptized, it would be nice to say that the process is complete—that we will never sin again. The truth is that we do sin again. The law of God may reign in our mind, but unless we are purer than Paul, ''the law of sin is at work in my members." Rm 7:23 As long as we are in this body of flesh and blood, we are subject to doing wrong things. The spirit may be willing, but the flesh is weak.

The problem of post-baptismal sin—sinning after we have been baptized—has been a stumbling block from the beginning. We must know that God has dealt with post-baptismal sin and all other sin in Jesus Christ. This was part of the revelation that led Paul to write, "There is now, therefore no condemnation for those who are in Christ Jesus." Rm 8:1 He was aware that there was still sin. He saw it in himself as well as other Christians. What he knew was that God was not going to condemn us while He was in the process of making us into new creatures. The things that we do wrong while we are learning to walk in the Spirit will not be charged against us by God—or by anyone who is in Christ Jesus.

I used to rejoice over this scripture when other people would condemn me for my teaching. I could not be touched by them because I was in Christ. I would then condemn them for condemning me. I used it as a shield from which I could fight. One day the Lord spoke to me about it. "Son, if you are going to condemn, you are not in Christ Jesus. In Him condemnation is neither given nor received." Another look at the scripture showed me what it meant. I can no longer use it as a cover while I condemn others. When I do condemn others, I am not in Christ Jesus.

There are a variety of ways to handle post-baptismal sin. Some people argue that when they are saved and filled with the Holy Spirit, they cannot sin. They then conclude that nothing they do is sinful. That allows them to use their freedom as a cloak for license. Until they realize that they can still sin, they are not open to continued growth in Jesus Christ.

Others repress their sin until it manifests in some other way. They deny their feelings of pride or lust or anger or whatever. They push them down into the heart where they bring forth fruit in their body as sickness or some abnormal behavior. This practice generally leads to split level living. I am one person when I am with the brethren, but I do other things when no one is looking. Growth is bound until we learn to confess our sins instead of repress our sins. God does not want to condemn, but to heal.

When I made my first commitment to Jesus and received forgiveness of my sins, it lasted for a brief time only. When I finally realized that I had blown the whole thing, I decided that I might as well live like I had blown it.

It was not until someone told me that Jesus loved me with an unconditional love that any hope was restored. I found that Jesus did forgive again and again and again. He demonstrated to me in my own life what He had told Peter—seventy times seven times. Jesus not only forgave all that I had done; but he forgave all that I am going to do tomorrow. That is not license to sin; it is freedom to continue seeking a new life in Jesus when I have sinned.

We should not sin that grace may abound. That is not the purpose of Jesus' death. It would mean that we were not seeking change in our inner life. We are going to sin, so we thank God that His grace does abound. We do not seek to avoid sin because we are afraid that we won't be forgiven; we avoid sin because it is stupid. It is contrary to God's purpose for us, and it detracts from our joy and peace. We are not punished FOR our sins; we are punished BY our sins.

I do not regret the experience of being lost. I know what the world sets forth as the "good life," and I know it is hell. It carries despair and pain, loneliness and fear that promise death with no promise of resurrection. That is Satan's way. He makes the promise of fulfillment, but he delivers only empty dreams. By the time I heard the gospel, I was ready to try anything. The best that I could find in the world was still hell.

There is no desire on my part to go back to the world's ways. There are from time to time reactions that come from old feelings that need to be healed when they arise. I have learned to seek healing as the need surfaces from my heart. There are occasional compulsions that arise contrary to my will. I have learned to seek exorcism where it is needed. In that way I can use the goad that Satan uses against me in the flesh. I can make it an occasion of death to that flesh and resurrection to new life.

I must confess that without the devil, I would likely fail to grow very much. I tend to be a lazy Christian. As long as things are in tolerable condition, I put off seeking the continued growth to which God has called us. Fortunately, Satan leaves me little time to rest. He goads me on through tribulation toward the love whereby Jesus has overcome the world.

I long for the day when Satan has finally destroyed all of the flesh in me, and I can live unmolested in the presence of God. That day shall come. It is God's promise. Until then I can walk my pilgrimage knowing that I will meet Satan and every obstacle he has to throw in my way. I also know that every stumbling block he sets for me can be a stepping stone toward my perfection in the Kingdom of God.

The Occult
Confusion, Fascination, and Bondage

THE OCCULT HAS ALWAYS been a source of fascination to some people, but a source of fear to others. The occult is the realm of Satan. It lies totally within the realm of the old creation, and it is the devil's hunting ground for souls. It is in shadow hidden from sight. It is the spiritual context of hidden forces in the creation. It is a realm that promises excitement and fulfillment; but the promise is an illusion of the prince of darkness of this world.

The occult has neither part nor parcel with the new creation. The occult powers have no access to the new creation nor to the people who live in the new creation. Satan no longer stands before the throne of God day and night accusing the brethren. Satan has fallen like lightning in the face of the authority that Jesus has given to the Church.

In the old creation Satan has set forth a counterfeit kingdom of gods. It uses the same language. It promises perfection in a land of peace. It promises fulfillment of man's will—everything he wants. It follows a way to perfection that is called holiness but it is a hidden way—a way of secret knowledge. It is a way that must be learned from other masters that have learned it through revelation. It is a way of incantation, sorcery, witchcraft and wizardry. It is a way in which man is the one who determines the way of history, and those who are stronger control those who are weaker.

This is totally contrary to the Lord Jesus Christ who is the Way. In Jesus, the Way is no secret; the Way is not hidden. It is not a matter of man seeking God to manipulate Him. It is God seeking man in order that He might love him. It is this open Kingdom of love wherein God's will is done; and all men live in that will. That is the kingdom that Satan has tried to distort. There is a vast difference in my will being subjected to God's will; and my trying to make God's will subject to mine.

We are neither to fear the occult nor mistake it for empty superstition. It is real. It is in a realm that is passing away, but it is real. It is with us from birth to death; but it has no grace and cannot give life. There is power in the occult, but it has no claim on the spirit of a Christian. It might destroy the flesh, but only to the salvation of the spirit. There is no ground in the Christian where it might stand, except in the flesh. It might hit or hurt or hassle; but it cannot bind the new creature because it has no place in the new creation. It might well be a nuisance to the Christian, but it can never be a mortal threat.

Anyone who is seeking to walk in the Kingdom of God might as well leave the occult alone. It can be of no help to those who are seeking guidance for the Kingdom because it has no knowledge of the Kingdom. While it may give guidance to those who live in the old creation, it is not even the best guide for that purpose. It was not Satan who created all things but God. When we have received the Holy Spirit, we have access to all of the wisdom of God. We have all that we need to walk in both the old and the new.

There is a confusion of spirit in the old creation. There is a claim made by many spirits to be the Holy Spirit. They can even manifest power and miracle. They will lead many astray who put their trust in power or miracle; but they cannot counterfeit love. These are the spirits who are separated from God, and through the ages have led man away from God as we know Him in Jesus Christ.

The realm of the occult is the realm of rebellion against God. It promises man that he can attain mastery over the material world through the use of hidden powers. The price that man pays is his own soul. In order to take advantage of Satan's promise, I must reject the promise that God has made in Jesus. We cannot serve both God and mammon. It is the arena where man might choose to pit his own wit and will against God in God's own creation. It requires only that man yield himself to some spirit other than the Holy Spirit.

The great Sin of the occult is idolatry. It is setting other gods before the one true and living God. It is in this area that both the Old and the New Testaments show concern. It is in the realm of guidance that the condemnation of the occult is found. Leviticus is clear about the issue. ''Do not turn to mediums or wizards.'' Lev 19:31 ''If a person turns to mediums and wizards, playing the harlot after them, I will set my face against that person and will cut him off.'' Lev 20:6 Finally it is written, ''A man or woman who is a medium or wizard shall be put to death; they shall be stoned with stones, their blood shall be upon them.'' Lev 20:27

Deuteronomy sets the prohibition in the context of teaching about the proper source of guidance. ''There shall not be found among you . . . anyone who practices divination, a soothsayer, or an augur, or a sorcerer, or a charmer, or a medium, or a wizard, or a necromancer. For whoever does these things is an abomination to the Lord . . . The Lord your God will raise up for you a prophet like me from among you, from your brethren—him shall you heed.'' Deut 18:10ff

The concern seems to be that the people of God get their guidance straight from God rather than seeking it through lesser spirits. Isaiah speaks from this viewpoint when he says, ''When they say to you, 'Consult the mediums and wizards who chirp and utter,' should not a people consult their God? Should they consult the dead on behalf of the living?'' Isa 8:19

Jeremiah points out the same kind of apostasy when he says, ''. . . for my people have committed two evils: they have forsaken me, the fountain of living waters, and hewed out cisterns for themselves, broken cisterns, that can hold no water.'' Jer 2:13   The concern is once more that Israel has settled for less than God has for them, in pursuing other gods.

Other nations do not have the option. They consult their own gods in whatever way they can. That is the best that they have to go with. That is not so with Israel. In all of the old creation, Israel and Judah are the only people who have access to the one who created all things. Israel and Judah alone stand as some form of inbreaking of the Kingdom that is to be brought to fruition by Jesus.

The King of Babylon uses divination, the shaking of arrows, the teraphim, and looking at sheep's liver to determine whether to attack Jerusalem or Rabah, of the Ammonites. The lot fell to Jerusalem, but the people were deceived into thinking that it was some false divination. The whole deal comes out as God calls the turn—even for those who are not His people. God is in control, and He intends to support a people who will accept that control and seek Him alone as their God. Ezek 21:21ff

Christians share somewhat the same position in the world as was shared by the Jews. We have access to the throne of grace through Jesus Christ. We are born into a new creation through His sacrifice. We receive it through His grace. We have no need to consult spirits that are able to give us half truths at best. We are the new Israel, and we are called to heed only the voice of God. This is our key to understanding the place of the occult and the nature of its reality in the creation of God.

Many people get involved with the occult as a parlor game. They do not take it seriously. It is an enticement especially to the curious. Whether they are aware of its reality or not, the power of the occult is still present. It will bind anyone who gives it the opportunity. There is no distinction between the knowledgeable and the ignorant. Both are fair game to the spirits of darkness.

Once hooked by the spiritual power of the occult, the subject may well be in bondage and be unaware of that bondage. If they try to find freedom through the use of the occult, they might well be set free by another spirit of the occult only to come into a deeper bondage. They may use incantations and spells and props to move spirits in the occult realm; but it is much like moving fly paper from one hand to another in an effort to get rid of it. The only real way to freedom lies in the power of the Name of Jesus. It is in His cross that the power of the occult was broken.

I have a close friend who became involved with astrology. She was far beyond the newsstand variety of horoscope. She had purchased books valued in the neighborhood of $3,000 to pursue her quest for knowledge and power through that knowledge. She did not know that she was in bondage. I had talked to her about the life of the Spirit, and about the realm of Satan; but she was not able to hear. She understood her psychic talent as a gift from God. It was given to her that she might map the destiny of those around her—to be in some way a messiah herself.

Prayer has the capacity to bring confrontation. Her son was praying in his bedroom one night and the Holy Spirit came into his life in power. He knew the problems that his mother had; and his prayer brought her face to face with the demonic power with which she was involved in the use of astrology. What she heard while she washed her dishes one day was, ''Tonight your soul will be required of you.'' That was enough to get her attention. She sought the prayers of those she knew who prayed. She received deliverance from the Dean of a nearby cathedral; and she spent the night in terror until she was able to renounce Satan and call for Jesus to come into her life as Savior. He came to deliver her from terror to peace. The spirit that had been pressing on her was banished from her house.

One of the common toys with a widespread demand today is the ouija board. It is a board with letters and numbers and a little planchette, a small triangular table which sits on the board. The participant sits with fingers on the planchette with their hands yielded to whatever spirit happens along. Questions are asked and the answer is spelled out on the board. When I was a child, we had one. I was willing to yield my hands to the use of the spirits; and I was open enough to half believe the answers. I was also fortunate enough to have God keep me safe. That has not been true of all ouija board users.

Another manifestation of the occult that falls into the same category is automatic writing. It requires that we yield our hand holding pen or pencil, to any spirit that might happen along. The spirit uses our hand to write messages to us. We can ask questions and get answers; but we have to yield control of a portion of our body. It was a popular practice among the curious some years ago.

My first encounter with someone who had gotten into severe difficulty by trying the discipline occurred one evening when I received a call that came out of sheer desperation. It was from a woman who had not been able to sleep for three nights, and who was torn within by a multitude of feelings at war with each other. Someone had told her that I might be able to help her, and so she drove some distance to seek help.

As she had begun the practice of automatic writing, the first spirit she encountered seemed rather benign. She continued the practice, and the second and third spirits were pornographic and suicidal. They made demands on her for the use of her body. On one hand she felt that she wanted to appear and act ''sexy,'' and on the other hand she wanted to kill herself. The total chaos within her was apparent from her outward appearance.

The battle for her body was not an easy one. She had yielded voluntarily to the spirits; and the spirits did not want to relinquish what they had been given. They wanted to squeeze all of the trauma they could from her. They wanted to control the thinking and feeling and the decisions. They wanted to displace the woman from her own body if that was possible. We won the battle in the Name of Jesus; and the woman decided that it might be a good idea for her to make a commitment to Him rather than the spiritual world in general. He became her Savior and her Lord.

The experience was not bad in the final analysis. There may have been an easier way for the woman to come to Jesus Christ as Lord; but the fact is that she did not take one of the easier ways. She began with a search for truth, and she found the Truth. She did not find Him where she had been looking— in the occult realm—but He had found her there, and led her out. It was through her bondage to the occult that she was driven to Jesus.

I would not recommend this path to anyone else. I believe there are easier ways to find Jesus. I would, however, recommend the last few steps to everyone. I highly recommend the renunciation of the occult, the deliverance from bondage, and the affirmation of Jesus as Savior and Lord.

The important thing to know about ouija and automatic writing is they are not just games. There is a reality behind them that is unseen. It is a spiritual power that uses all anyone will give to it. If I allow any such spirit to use me, the spirit might well take advantage of the situation and abuse me. There is nothing to be gained but a little entertainment; and there is much to be lost in the experience.

Tarot cards do not present the same kind of menace as the ouija for those who play with them. The body is not yielded to a possession relationship with some spirit. The cards are yielded rather than the body. It is through the cards that the spirits communicate. The danger of the Tarot is that they can give enough guidance to mislead those who begin to take them seriously. It is an easy matter to place one's self in bondage to the cards simply by using them as a hope to gain knowledge of the future.

Men have always had a curiosity about the future. They want to know it so they can seek to control it—at least that part to which they are directly related. They want to know so they can prepare themselves to meet the events of tomorrow. Thus they look to the stars or cards or spirits of some kind to open the secrets of the future. There are some who do not understand prophecy as forth telling. They want it to be foretelling. They want to be able to go to anyone who has been called a prophet for answers for tomorrow. They treat him as some sort of holy ouija board.

The future is not set. That which is prophesied does not have to come true. There is always an option. The Old Testament prophets tried to make clear that repentence would avert disaster; they just didn't find very much repentence. The prophecy about Hezekiah was that he was to die. Hezekiah repented, and petitioned God for mercy. Hezekiah's life was extended fifteen years in spite of the prophecy. It was not a matter of false prophecy; it was matter of a repentent person.

Foreknowledge is often given to the people of God so that they might use it to inform their prayers. Anyone who has read about the experience of Agnes Sanford is struck by this reality. She was led by God to move to the San Andreas fault in California to pray for the healing of the land. All of the prophets—both Pentecostal and occult—were certain that an earthquake was going to drop California into the ocean. I would not say that Agnes saved California, or that the prophecy was wrong. I would simply say that foreknowledge of disaster is a call to intercession.

There is a widespread popular interest in astrology today. There is an astrology section in nearly every daily newspaper with little horoscopes for the day. There are many who read these religiously before they begin the day. They will assert that they don't really believe in them. They just want to see what they say; but within there is that little hope that they might get a little peep into the future. Any newsstand yields a multitude of magazines which tell you in greater detail what you might expect for your life. If you are really serious, you can invest thousands in books as my friend of whom we wrote above.

The promise of a horoscope is that we can read tomorrow's news today. There is enough truth in astrology to mislead those who are seeking guidance. The first gentiles to worship Jesus were astrologers. They were led to the child by the star that went before them. Even when they had conferred with Herod and had the prophecy, they were led by the star. It went before them to stand over the place where the child was living.

The problem with using astrology is that it is idolatry. It is putting something else before God. It is worshipping the creation instead of the Creator. If we have no intention of walking in the Kingdom of God, we might elect astrology as a guidance system. I suppose it is as good as any other substitute for God. To anyone who wants to walk in the Kingdom, it is useless. There is no way to calculate an astrological chart for someone who is born again into a new creation unknown to the spirits of the stars.

Few people today are tempted to use augury or looking at the entrails of a chicken for their guidance. There are much neater means than opening an animal to examine various parts of the anatomy. It would never become widely used in the United States; the Society for the Prevention of Cruelty to Animals would raise a cry against it.

There is an increasing practice in the world of witchcraft and Satanism. They are closely related in that they yield to Satan and his lieutenants in the spiritual world. They make an effort to control the unseen forces in the spiritual world for personal gain. In order to become a witch or a Satanist, there is an initiatory rite in which the novice offers his body to be used by the prevailing spirit of the coven of witches or congregation of Satanists.

The excitement of sex and drug involvement in the name of religion is an intriguing idea to those who are exposed to witchcraft or Satanism. The idea that power is available to get one's will done is even more enticing to those who are drawn into the web. Much of what passes for witchcraft remains at this level. There are few truly powerful witches because it takes as much discipline to be truly evil as it does to be truly good.

Once a person has yielded his body to a possessing spirit, that one is hooked. He remains hooked unless and until Jesus sets him free. Forces are at work which leave them at the mercy of the spirits, and at the mercy of those who are more powerful in the occult than they. Spells, incantations, and convenants with the spiritual realm through blood and sex wield real power over those who are not under the protection of the new convenant in Jesus blood.

When anyone seeks to control the power that is in the hands of Satan, he is also controlled by that power. The covenant with hell works both ways. The authority and power will be made available to those who will worship Satan; but the power will also bind the one who wields it. This was the temptation that Jesus recognized and refused. ''Thou shalt worship the Lord thy God, and Him only shalt thou serve.''

A young girl who had been the female leader in a Satanist cult was brought to my parish so that I might assist in the exorcism. We had worked with the girl before, and the spirit was too strong for one person to contend with while trying to control the body of the girl at the same time. When she was in her own mind, she told us she wanted to be free. She had known Jesus in some way at one time, but she had been led into the cult by her attachment with a boy. Once there she was hooked. When we began to pray, all hell literally broke loose. She was driven by the strength of that supernatural spirit within her. She was slight in stature, but it was still a chore to hold her. In the end, the power of Jesus prevailed, and the girl was set free. It was not just a simple case of a single spirit. It was a multiple possession by spirits who wanted to use her body for their own pleasure.

Follow up ministry was needed for her continued healing. No one is ever healed by exorcism; it just removes the cause of the illness. Healing comes through the positive growth of the person in the power of God through the indwelling of the Holy Spirit. The inner voids that are created by the exorcism need to be filled. That which is planted needs time to grow. The inner life of the person must integrate and find its center in Jesus Christ. That is both our healing and our protection.

When a strong man keeps his place, his goods are in safety; but when a stronger one comes, he takes him captive and takes the spoils for himself. When a person is rid of an unclean spirit of some kind, the Holy Spirit is invited in to take and to hold the spoils (us). He binds the one who holds us captive and He takes us for His own.

Some people do not believe that they need the Holy Spirit when they are exorcised. They feel that they can handle things themselves once they get free. Jesus taught us that it was necessary to fill the house so that it might not remain empty. "When the unclean spirit has gone out of a man, he passes through waterless places seeking rest; and finding none he says, 'I will return to my house from which I came.' And when he comes he finds it swept and put in order. Then he goes and brings seven other spirits more evil than himself, and they enter and dwell there; and the last state of that man becomes worse than the first." Lk 11:24-26

When I first became involved in exorcism, I had that happen to one of the people to whom I was ministering. We worked through the emptying process, and finally reached the point where we felt that she was clean. I suggested that we pray for the infilling of the Holy Spirit; but she insisted that she didn't want to be crazy like "those other people." Within three months she was in a sanitarium. The next time I saw her was at a retreat center. She was seeking to be delivered and filled with the Holy Spirit. Since that time, I do not work with people who are not willing to seek the Lord to occupy that ground that we gain through exorcism.

God is not a magician or illusionist; He is a Creator. He created all things; and at our invitation, He will make us a new creation. As we pointed out in the last chapter it is a process. It will not happen in the twinkling of an eye unless it happens to be the last day. It will be growth as He brings us from glory to glory. The occult will offer you freedom to do your will in the power of the old creation, and it will bring you into bondage. Jesus calls us to slavery to the living God, and it will set us free to walk in the perfect freedom of His service.

The occult does not operate in honesty. It sometimes puts on masks so that "the angel of darkness appears in the congregation as the angel of light." II Cor 11:14 Any self righteous judgment that we make of what is good and evil is occult. Any teaching of prayer techniques to get God to do what we will is occult. Any effort to make a prophet answer our questions about the future is occult. It takes the initiative out of God's hands and seeks to wield them as men.

The truth is that the only areas of our lives which are not occult are those which are made new and centered in a personal relationship with Jesus Christ. We are set free only as we seek first God's Kingdom and His righteousness. It was as man received the capacity for moral judgment that he fell. As we continue to usurp God's perogative to judge good and evil, we remain in the old creation. We remain in bondage to the occult.

There are many who lay claim to godliness today because of the power they wield. They speak of the souls they have saved, the sick they have healed, the possessed they have delivered, and the prophecy they have spoken as proofs of the work of the Holy Spirit in their lives. It is hard for us to believe that God would use someone who was not really Godly; but Paul was not deceived by human logic. He knew and he wrote that love, and not power is the measure of the Christian life. All of the power in the universe will not profit a man without love.

Rebellion is as witchcraft. That is what happened to Saul. Jesus met that temptation on the pinacle of the temple. "Cast your self down if you are the Son of God." It sounds like such a good idea that we might try it if we thought we could pull it off. Jesus' reply was, "Thou shalt not tempt the Lord thy God." It is not up to us to decide what is good and evil. It is up to us to live in communion and communication with the living God. It is up to us to yield to His will that it might be done on earth as it is in heaven.

Those who intentionally seek to follow the occult to the ultimate end, will find their own hell. It is given to the occult to destroy the flesh. It was for that reason Paul admonished the Corinthian Church to turn one of the brethren over to Satan. "You are to deliver this man to Satan for the destruction of the flesh, that his spirit may be saved in the day of the Lord Jesus." I Cor 5:5 Satan is to have his way with all that he has access to so that he might destroy it; but Paul is still concerned over the spirit of the brother he has had cast into the teeth of the occult.

Deliverance comes when we begin to experience both sides of the issue. We need to renounce the devil and all his works. We need to be ready to die to the world as we know it. We affirm Jesus as Savior and Lord. That is where the ground is taken from beneath the feet of Satan and brought into the new creation. It may also take a command in the Name of Jesus to any spirit or any spell to release the one who is bound. That is simply exercising the authority that God has given us in Jesus—to tread upon serpents and scorpions, but not upon men.

Where deliverance seems difficult, we persevere knowing that we have been set free by the blood of Jesus. The web that has been woven by the occult powers may be complex indeed; but as we seek the Holy Spirit's guidance, He will lead us through the maze of deceit to manifest the glory of our God.

Our authority does not lie in our knowledge about the demonic; nor does it lie in the techniques that we use to deal with the demonic. It lies in the presence and power of God. It lies in our yielding to Him to be led, and to be used as an instrument of His reconciliation. It is in our allowing Jesus to be in us and through us for others to set them free.

There is nothing to fear in the occult. That does not mean that we play games with occult power. If we do, we will get hurt. It is much the same as walking in traffic. I am not afraid to walk in traffic; but I don't do it because that is not a profitable place to walk. I walk on sidewalks because they were made for that purpose.

New knowledge that there are forces surrounding us that we cannot see need not frighten us. They were there yesterday, and did not frighten us. I have seen many who panicked when they first found out about the demonic. Panic and fear merely open doors for their operation. We need rather deal with them in the love of God casting out each one in His time and in His way; and seeking the indwelling power of the Holy Spirit to establish us as the Temple of God wherein no demon can enter.

Spiritualism

T HE PRACTICE OF SPIRITUALISM lies in the realm of the occult. It is of the old creation. I elected to deal with it separately because it claims to deal with a particular kind of spirit, and as a rule does not seek to wield occult power. Its major power lies in the information that it receives from that source. It is an effort to contact some loved one that has entered the larger life or to find some information that is not readily available to the living.

It is not a new phenomenon. It is as old as man, and is responsible for many of the taboos that surround the dead in religions of man. The way in which the Jews dealt with the dead in Biblical times is indicative of the fact that it had influence on Biblical faith. There is an explicit direction about handling the dead and the places where they die and the things around them in Num 19:11 and following. There is an elaborate way for purifying the people and it is mandatory that it be done right. If the requirements are not met, the unclean person is cut off from the people.

There is a strong probability that the Jews picked up from their neighbors the idea that the spirits of the dead might come back to take up living in the body of a living person. This seems likely in their treatment of the departed; and in Hebrew folklore there are stories about the dibbuks—the spirits of the departed who have returned to plague the living. This would be called in some cases a familiar spirit. They had to take care that they did not become a carrier if they hoped to stay within the community.

It is not unusual for people all over the world, and even in this country to experience the presence of people who have recently died. The experience might be accounted for by seeing it as a strong psychological longing to see the person, or some mental stress. The experience is common enough for us to at least recognize that it is a possibility that it is a reality. I have a very good friend who is aware of the presence of her husband when she is at worship on Sunday. It is this communion of saints in the worship of God that is counterfeited by spiritualism.

Josephus, the ancient Jewish historian believed with many other Jews that the demons that buffeted men were spirits of evil men who had departed the flesh but could find no rest. Many of the early Christian fathers believed that some of the spirits came from the offspring of the Sons of God and the daughters of men—the giants of Genesis 6.

The laws against necromancy indicated that the people thought it possible to contact the dead. Since the scripture is inspired by God, we must either say that necromancy is a possibility or that God prohibited something that is not possible anyway. The prohibitions are clearly in the area of the people seeking guidance from the dead since God has promised to speak to His people through a prophet that He will raise up from their midst.

The passage from Isaiah that mentions this type of communication that was used by the governments of the nations surrounding Israel for guidance. When the Lord does not speak to the House of Jacob, Isaiah says, "When they shall say unto you, 'Seek unto them that have familiar spirits, and unto wizards that peep, and that mutter,' should not a people seek their God? Should they consult the dead on behalf of the living?'' Isa 8:19

This is the thing that Saul did when God had cut him off. When he could no longer get a word from the Lord, he turned to something that would give him a word. Saul was desparate. We cannot imagine the fear that gripped him. We do our own planning without consulting God for the most part. In those days kings and leaders sought a word from their gods. Without it man had no way in which to receive support from the spiritual realm. The kings were not seen so much as being humans with wisdom of their own. They were the images of the gods who had oversight of the nation. Without a word from some god there was no hope.

Since the Lord would not speak to Saul, he went to the next best source. He sought out a woman who had a familiar spirit so he could consult Samuel. He went in disguise so that she might call Samuel for him. In his better days, Saul had cleansed the land of all who practiced necromancy or other arts of divination. Those who were detected in the land were killed in accord with the law. "A man also or woman that hath a familiar spirit, or that is a wizard, shall surely be put to death: they shall stone them with stones." Lev 20:27

When Saul came to the woman, he came at night. He could not afford to have anyone see him. He said, "Divine for me by a spirit, and bring up for me whomever I shall name to you."

The woman answered, "Surely you know what Saul has done, how he has cut off the mediums and the wizards from the land. Why then are you laying a snare for my life to bring about my death?'' The woman obviously was out of practice, and did not want to hold a seance. She seems to have been quite a compassionate woman who was willing to be obedient to the law.

Saul reassured her by swearing to her by the Lord, ''As the Lord lives, no punishment shall come upon you for this thing.''

The woman finally relented. ''Whom shall I bring up for you?''

''Bring up Samuel for me,'' was the reply.

The woman began her trance to call up Samuel; but when she saw him she was terrified. ''Why have you deceived me? You are Saul.''

Saul tried to assure her again. ''Have no fear; what do you see?''

The woman answered Saul, ''I see a god coming up out of the earth.''

''What is his appearance?''

''An old man is coming up; and he is wrapped in a robe.''

Saul knew that it was Samuel, and he bowed with his face to the ground and did obeisance. There are some who do not like to face the fact that the Bible says that this was in fact Samuel. They argue that it looked like Samuel to deceive Saul. The custodians of scripture were not near as concerned about it being Samuel as are their modern brethren. The scripture is clear; and it seems that the spirit was quite in keeping with Samuel. If Samuel had been there in the flesh, he would have said the same thing. He was not solicitous of Saul as a deceiver would have been. He was honest and straight forward. The scriptures insist that it was the real thing.

Samuel reacted like the real Samuel. ''Why have you disturbed me by bringing me up?''

Saul answered out of his anguish. ''I am in great distress; for the Philistines are warring against me, and God has turned away from me and answers me no more, either by prophets or by dreams; therefore I have summoned you to tell me what I shall do.''

Then Samuel spoke to Saul. ''Why then do you ask me, since the Lord has turned from you and become your enemy? The Lord has done to you as he spoke by me; for the Lord has torn the kingdom out of your hand, and given it to your neighbor, David. Because you did not obey the voice of the Lord, and did not carry out his fierce wrath against Amalek, therefore the Lord has done this thing to you this day. Moreover the Lord will give Israel also with you into the hand of the Philistines; and tomorrow you and your sons will be with me; the Lord will give the army of Israel also into the hand of the Philistines.''

Saul's reaction would not lead us to believe that the spirit was anyone but Samuel. The words that the spirit spoke would not lead us to believe otherwise. It is not an argument for the use of spiritualism as a means for seeking guidance. It is simply an indication that the scriptures—right or wrong—believed it was possible to do so. Since it was idolatrous, it was forbidden.

Some years ago, a book called *The Challenging Counterfeit* was published and widely read in some Christian circles. The book was written by a man who had been a medium. His control spirit had been a departed witch doctor. When the medium wanted to be free from his control, the spirit tried to kill him. The result was that the medium concluded that it was not the spirit of a departed person, but a spirit masquerading as a departed spirit.

We cannot disagree with someone else's experience. Whatever happens to you is what happens. I cannot tell you that it did or did not. I know from my own experience that when people deny your witness, it is a form of spiritual murder. There have been many Christians who have been brought back into bondage by people who do not allow others their experience—who literally talk them out of it by psychologizing it.

It is not the witness of the author that seems to run amiss. It is his conclusions that all spiritualism deals solely with the demonic, and there are no human spirits wandering the earth seeking rest. It seems to me that this is allowed first by scripture, and is supported by the experience of men throughout history where the presence of ghosts in people and places has been known; and where the church has ministered to their rest.

There is, on the other hand, no scripture that states clearly that those who have departed have left the world unless it be those who have departed to be with Jesus. Even these are in the communion of saints who are related to us in Jesus as we worship before the throne of God. We are one in Jesus Christ, and we cannot be separated from those who have entered the larger life in Him. It is this communion of saints that spiritualism counterfeits.

There is need to say that scripture prohibits us from seeking guidance from any source other than God Himself. It is the work of the Holy Spirit to lead us into all truth. There is no other spirit that can do that. For this reason we do not seek guidance from the dead. We seek guidance from the Holy Spirit instead of the departed or instead of those who are still with us in the flesh. There is little difference between letting our lives be directed by the departed or the living spirits of men. We are not even to follow our own minds and wills; we seek God's will. Seeking any other source of guidance is rebellion, and we know that rebellion is as witchcraft.

Deliverance from bondage to a control spirit, as they are called today, or familiar spirit as they were called in the Bible, is not simply a matter of casting out a demon. If indeed the spirit is a departed person, then we ought to deal with it in another way. Demons certainly do not need to be set free to enter the Kingdom of God; but neither do spirits of the departed need to be cast into hell. Jesus made it clear that the gates of hell should not prevail against the Church. We are called to empty the storehouse of lost souls—even as Jesus gave us example in His own ministry.

We read in the third and fourth chapters of I Peter, "Christ also died for sins once for all, the righteous for the unrighteous, that he might bring us to God, being put to death in the flesh but made alive in the spirit; in which he went and preached to the spirits in prison, who formerly did not obey, when God's patience waited in the days of Noah, during the building of the ark, in which a few, that is, eight persons, were saved through water. Baptism, which corresponds to this, now saves you, not as a removal of dirt from the body but as an appeal to God for a clear conscience, through the resurrection of Jesus Christ, who has gone to heaven and is at the right hand of God, with angels, authorities, and powers subject to him." I Pet 3:18-22

Since Christ suffered in the flesh, so ought we. We must die to sin in the flesh so that we might live with God in the Spirit. Our unbelieving friends might not accept our change in lifestyle, since we will not continue to run with them. They will likely put us down as being fanatics. Even though they are unaware of the presence and the power of the risen Christ, it is they, "Who will give account to him who is ready to judge the living and the dead. For this is why the gospel was preached even to the dead, that though judged in the flesh like men, they might live in the spirit like God." I Pet 4:5-6

Paul is aware of the practice in the Corinthian church of baptizing for the dead. Paul said nothing against it or for it, so you can take your choice about how he felt about it. He simply used it in the discussion of the resurrection. "Otherwise, what do people mean by being baptized on behalf of the dead? If the dead are not raised at all, why are people baptized on their behalf?" I Cor 15:29

If we are to be involved in the ministry of Jesus, then we are called to preach to the departed as well as to the living. That is what He did when He descended into hell during His three days between crucifixion and resurrection. This is a hard saying for those who want to rid themselves of the spirits of the dead as soon as they die. For those who believe that we are truly to empty hell by the proclamation and power of the gospel, it is an opportunity. If Jesus Christ is the same yesterday, today, and forever, then the ministry that He once had to the departed continues.

One of the great doctrines of evangelical Christianity is that we must make our decision for Jesus in this life or we will be damned for the rest of eternity. I find no scripture that states that clearly, and I find as much that can be interpreted to say otherwise. I know only that it is God's will that ALL men be saved. That is His proclamation in Jesus Christ. It is the purpose for the death of Christ. I cannot believe that God changes His mind about us when we die.

It would seem that the reason for the belief lies in our own concern that people not put off their decision for Jesus. We will do anything to get them to make that decision—even use fear. The reason for deciding today is that I might be a partaker of the Kingdom now instead of having to wait. Anyone who has a desire to put off their decision for Jesus doesn't really want to go to heaven anyway. They just want to avoid hell; but they think the world is a better place than the Kingdom or they would decide now for Jesus. I suspect there are many who will not find joy in the Kingdom because they have not really chosen Kingdom life. They will back into the Kingdom and find that it is not at all what they expected.

With this realization, it is evident that the major error of spiritualism is that they seek to communicate in the wrong direction. It is not a matter of our seeking guidance in the wrong direction. It is not a matter of our seeking guidance from the dead, or even comfort from them. It is a call to preach the gospel to the dead as Jesus did so that they might be reconciled. There are many who die out of relationship to God. These people need to hear the gospel, and they need to be forgiven. They need to be set free to get on with their life in the Kingdom of God.

Some of these spirits find access to bodies that are not their own. I do not know how this is true, but I do know that the Jews were aware of the danger as we pointed out before. I also know in the religion of Tibet, the Dalai Lama is to be found in the body of the next child born after he dies. I have found much the same thing in people with whom I have dealt.

The first time I read of the idea was in a tract written by George Bennett, a well known warden of a healing home in England. There was a young nun who came to him because she was bothered by a spirit. When they had talked and prayed, it appeared to be the spirit of a young chap who had been befriended by the nun, and who had been killed in the war.

The spirit spoke to him through the girl. He had not known what to do when he had been killed, and so he sought out the one in whom he had seen a measure of loving concern. The young man had been an atheist. Father Bennett preached the gospel to him, and forgave him his sins. He then sent him to Jesus. The spirit said, "Oh, you mean the shining one." When he had been assured that he was right, and that it was all right for him to go, he left the girl and never bothered her again.

There are many who seem to be inadvertant mediums. They are the ones with whom this form of deliverance seems to work. The story of George Ritchey recorded in his book *Return From Tomorrow* tells of seeing the same type of thing happen on the other side of death. In his journey, he saw a bar where men were in various degrees of drunkeness. There were a lot of figures, but some were not able to raise a glass. When one of the real ones passed out, one of the others slipped into his body. There he finally had a body that he could use to enjoy the drink that he lived for.

It would seem that many of the schizophrenics of this world are people who are indeed two people in one body. There may be other explanations for the disease, but this would seem to be one of them. The symptoms of this state of indwelling would be mild ambivalence—being of two minds—or of standing outside one's self from time to time. It might mean being two completely different personalities. It might mean doing things as one person that are not even remembered by the other.

Just recently a friend of mine was blessing a house, while he was blessing it, his wife spoke with a voice that was not hers. "You cannot bless this house. This is not your house." The message was delivered; and after a time the spirit left the body of the wife. The wife was able to remember the face of the spirit—she had an impression of what the person had looked like in the flesh. She later identified a picture that was there as the person whose spirit she knew. It was the deceased mother of the wife in the household.

In addition to that spirit, there was also one that my friend saw in his peripheral vision. He recognized the spirit as being another member of the family who had entered the larger life. It was almost as if they did not want the house blessed because they wanted to live there with the family. They had found the ultimate meaning of life in their family, and did not want to give it up for God.

The gospel was preached to the spirits for a week, and they were urged to go to Jesus and find the place that had been prepared for them. He absolved them from any sin, explained that God would not impose anything on them— He waits until we are willing to receive His gifts. The spirits finally left— presumably to go to Jesus.

Our experience tells us that we have a ministry to spiritualist followers who are seeking guidance from the dead. The door is open for us to preach the gospel to the dead—not receive information from them. The spiritualist talks about Jesus as the greatest medium that ever lived. They were right. That is the highest thing they can say from their viewpoint. Jesus was a medium; and we are called to be mediums with the same control Spirit He had.

When Jesus was baptized, He was given the Holy Spirit to lead Him into obedience in the flesh. He was already obedient in the spirit. Our control Spirit leads us into all truth. He gives us contact with the only departed person who is the Truth. He is the one to whom we open our lives that He might control us as we yield to Him. He acts in us in much the same way a familiar spirit acts in a medium. He will not impose His will on us. We must ask; but when we ask, He does not impose but enable.

It is this relationship that is counterfeited by spiritualist mediums. It is this relationship they claim in the name of some other spirit. There can be no counterfeit unless there is something worth counterfeiting. The spiritualist has settled for something less than the Kingdom of God because he is confused about God.

We cannot begin with our attention set on man, and wind up with God in proper relationship. We must begin with our attention focused on God, and He will reveal the truth about man. The Church has said little or nothing to the spiritualist culture. They have either considered spiritualism superstitious nonsense, or they have been so fearful that they have cut them off with unlistening condemnation. Their need is the same as ours. They need to be loved as Jesus loves them. They need to hear the gospel of the control Spirit that is able to bring truth out of their error.

Spiritualism is real. The people involved in it are in bondage that is real. That bondage cannot be broken through our withdrawal in our own fear. It can be broken only as we are willing to share the gospel in terms of their experience. We cannot justify casting anyone—in this life or the next—into hell. We are given power to break down the gates of hell that all men might be reconciled to the God who has given us that power in Jesus Christ.

Reincarnation
The Ultimate in Recycling

REINCARNATION IS ONE of the ancient theories of establishing moral justice. It grows out of two things. There is evidence in our experience that says nothing is fair in this life. There is a sense within that tells us God is fair. There must be some way to bring these two things together. Those who do not know Jesus Christ as the Savior of the world must find the answer in another way. The way many have found is in some theory of reincarnation.

Karma is the law that states there is a system of cause and effect in the spiritual world as well as the material world. In each case, the person who passes from one life to another will get his just desserts. If you messed up in your last cycle, then this one will be unpleasant. If you were good in your last life, then this one will be rewarding. What you sow in this life, you reap in the next.

It is clear to anyone who is familiar with the gospel at all, that reincarnation is totally contrary to the cross. It is in the cross of Jesus that I find the whole theory of reincarnation short circuited. There is no way that I can ever repay the debt that I owe for my sin. If I am perfect from now on, I cannot be better than perfect to make up for the past. Jesus has paid that debt for me. I am free to die with Him, and then receive from Him the gift of eternal life. I die once, and I am raised in a new body once. I die as a man of flesh; I am raised up a man of spirit. There is no recycling; there is just transformation.

God has dealt directly with me as a sinner. He has taken all of the steps necessary for me to be reconciled to Him. He has now opened the way for my perfection—not through what I do—through what He has done in Jesus. He has prepared his righteousness for me in Jesus. For this reason I am buried with Christ in His death, and I am raised up with Him in a new creation. That is not another try at getting it together in this world; it is a new life in God's eternal Kingdom. Such reality cuts the ground from any theory of reincarnation since such theories would be contrary to the revelation of God in Christ.

Those who believe in reincarnation do not believe in grace. They have not received the revelation of God in Christ. Since most of the world's religions begin with man seeking God, we should find that most of them will come up with some theory like reincarnation. Since the Judeo-Christian tradition is rooted in God seeking man, we are free to accept God's initiative in dealing with injustice. There is no trace of reincarnation among Christians who are rooted in the cross of Christ.

The Jewish faith has had to deal with the problem without the cross. Their origin grounded in God's choosing them to be His own, has led them to reject reincarnation as a rule—though some Jews do believe in it. The question of the suffering of the righteous is raised in the Book of Job. The final conclusion may be read in the story of the rich man and Lazarus as related by Luke's Gospel. Lazarus suffered on earth and was rewarded in the next life. The rich man enjoyed life on earth and suffered in the next.

Equity comes after death as God continues to deal with the issues. There is no reliance on a system of new births in new lives on earth for the purification of the soul. It is man's wisdom that developed the theory of reincarnation out of his own seeking and his own interpretation of his experience.

In order to deal with the experience of people who seem to have known and lived past lives, we have to make clear that reincarnation means that a soul comes back in its own body. If I come back into the world in someone else's body, that is not reincarnation but possession. Since one of the major arguments for belief in reincarnation is this residual memory, we must deal with alternatives that will let us understand it. For me to say it is not true because I have not had it is a form of spiritual murder.

My first encounter with someone who had an experience of a past life came through a girl in my congregation. She had been searching for some means to find stability for her life. She was not only an Episcopalian, but she was involved in many other spiritual groups. She had been taken back through regressive hypnotism to the memory of a young French girl of about two hundred years ago who was dying. On the basis of that experience, she believed that she was a reincarnation of that girl. I did not argue with the experience, I did take issue with the interpretation. In this case, I suggested that we try something to check it all out.

I was familiar with the case that George Bennett has related from England, and it sounded to me that this might be the same sort of situation. The girl was open to experimentation, and so we decided to preach the gospel to the girl who seemed to be present in my friend. We had reason to believe that the girl had not been baptized, which I thought unusual for a French girl, but we proceeded to baptize my friend for the spirit within. We dealt with the spirit as we would have dealt with someone in the flesh.

The spirit was absolved and told to go on to Jesus. With some continued urging, the spirit left. There was a physiological manifestation in my friend, coupled with a strong sense of departure of someone very close to her. The spirit or soul which held the memory of France was gone. Gone also was the great ambivalance that had plagued her. She was able to make peace with her mother; and she gave up all of her cult associations for Jesus Christ. Her reincarnation had not been reincarnation at all but possession.

Her experience was best explained as having a spirit that had once been in the flesh become incarnate in her flesh—not in flesh of its own. It was a matter of a spirit which was displaced and out of order because she did not know how to deal with life out of her own body on the other side of physical death. When she was put together with Jesus, absolved from her sin by the authority of the Church in accord with Jesus, and released from the body in which she was dwelling; she found the place that Jesus had for her. The girl in whose body she had been living found a new freedom that had not been hers before.

There have been a number of repeated experiences that bear witness to the same truth. The memories that I might have from a time before my birth were brought there by a spirit of whom they are a part; but they are not mine. As a matter of fact some multiple personalities can be dealt with through this type of deliverance, and often prebirth memories can be dealt with through this method.

It is truly more than a deliverance of a person from a spirit that seems to bind them. It is the deliverance of the indwelling spirit to go on with Jesus to its place in the Kingdom. When we are willing to wield the authority of Jesus, we are able to set men free from hell in this world and the next. That is not a matter of wishful thinking; it is the example of Jesus Himself.

Most of the people I have known and dealt with in this manner were easily delivered. Some of them are not so easy. There are some spirit visitors who are not so willing to leave. It then becomes a matter of using the spiritual authority over the old creation and do it by force. While it is better to bring a spirit into the new creation through the blood of Jesus, it is very important that we do not allow any spirit to keep a person confined in the old creation.

There are many who believe that human spirits could not be evil and therefore all spirits are evil spirits. This is the conclusion drawn by Raphael Gasson whom we mentioned in the chapter on Spiritualism. I must say that I have seen people that are capable of merciless treatment of others in the flesh, and I see no reason why they should change as they enter life on the other side. The only means of change it seems to me would be an encounter with the risen Lord. If I am possessed in the flesh, I might well be possessed in the spirit unless someone sets me free from bondage to walk in light.

I recently was called to help deal with a case of multiple personality compounded with demon possession of one of the persons. The case was analyzed by a secular therapist. All of the spirits within the person had been identified. He had been working with one of the persons at the conscious level when she suddenly went away and another person took the conscious level. When I was called the spirit which was in league with a demon was trying to take the body back to a coven of witches to be used for human sacrifice.

We prayed for the casting out of the demon and the reconciliation of the personality that was possessed. We further prayed to break some of the spirit control that had been there. The result was that the original personality could once more surface to resume her counselling relationship. I am not at all sure that we should not have gone further in dealing with the personalities, but we had worked with the girl for some time; and I felt led that what I had come to do had been done. From the last report I had, the demonic drive within the girl had been removed.

There is a sense in which a Christian can speak of reincarnation. The very heart of the Christian faith is the Incarnation of the Son of God. Jesus was the Word of God in our flesh. He was incarnate in the flesh of Mary His mother. If I seem to labor the point, it is because we often do not allow that point to sink into our heart.

When Jesus died, He was dead. He died in the same way that all men die— his body functions quit. He descended into hell. When He rose from the dead, He had a different body. It was not flesh and blood in the same way we are, it was transformed. His friends did not always recognize Him. He could walk through locked doors. He could leave Emmaus and travel to Jerusalem without walking. His body was different.

As we are open to the Holy Spirit, Jesus Christ is reincarnated in us. We become the flesh that He puts on. We are the Body of Christ. We are not simply a body in which the people of God dwell. We are the body in which God Himself dwells. In this sense, we believe in a kind of reincarnation. Indeed, it is this reincarnation that is able to remove the burden of sin that we have committed in the flesh. It comes in this form rather than the recycling of the human soul through countless births and deaths. This is the reality that the human theories of reincarnation seek to express.

The Christian faith does not believe in reincarnation in this world or any other; but we do believe in reimbodiment. Paul writes in his discussion of resurrection, "It is sown a physical body, it is raised a spiritual body." I Cor 15:44   We are not simply spirits that drift through eternity with no means of expression; we are persons who are born in the flesh, and given a new spiritual body as we enter into the new creation.

That is the reason we must be born again. That which is born of the flesh is flesh, and that which is born of the spirit is spirit. We are born into a new relationship to God as His children by adoption and grace. We are given a body of flesh as the children of the flesh; we are given a spiritual body as children of God who is Spirit. A spirit without a body is a ghost, and a body without a spirit is a corpse. We are called to be neither ghost nor corpse—but a new creature—a living being of body and spirit.

There is no evidence for us to believe that there are a series of lives that we must pass through after death as some would have us believe. There may be various levels of existence that we can pass through if we do not choose to live in Jesus; but there is one life that we enter in Him. That portion of the spiritual realm that lies outside the new creation must have its own heirarchy. There must be a way for them to say that there is a ladder toward perfection; but the message of the gospel is that we enter that eternal life with God now; and we grow into His perfection and not our own. There is no series of heavens through which we must pass. There is only a drawing to a closer relationship to our God whom we know NOW in Jesus, and with Whom we live in eternal life today.

There is another argument for reincarnation that rests in the experience called deja vu. It is the experience that we are living a script that we have lived before. We are in the same place that we have been before. There are times that people can walk into a place with the feeling that they know things about it that they have not been told. I would not argue that this experience is false; I have had a taste of it myself. I do not think that it means that we have been there before.

Generally when we argue this way, we assume that the place has never changed. I have never lived in a place for ten years that is not different from the way it was when I moved there. The foliage is different, the color is different, even the shape has sometimes been changed. Each time I have had the experience of being in a place before the feeling seemed to communicate that the place is still the same as it was then—there had been no change.

I once heard a psychological explanation of the experience in which it was pointed out that our senses informed our unconscious first, and when our conscious mind sought information about it from the unconscious, it was already there. My feeling then would be that I have already been there.

Another explanation of the experience might be that we do have a spirit within us that can reach out beyond us. We might well be entertaining a spirit that informs us of the very room that we are in without our having to see to touch it. Whatever we might use to explain the experience, we cannot call it a touch from a former life. In the former life the place would have been changed from what it appears to be today.

As we consider reincarnation or reembodiment through the resurrection of the dead, we face a problem. Those who do not know the risen Lord Jesus do not know the cleansing power of His blood. They are not aware of the complete freedom that God has prepared for us. They must find a way to explain how to pay for their own sins, and to make others pay for theirs.

It is not an easy out to believe in reincarnation. It is an entrapment wherein we seek and need a whole eternity to atone for our own sins. It is a distraction from the one source of atonement that God has given. It is a ground whereon men must strengthen their mastery over their own souls. It is a striving to come to perfection without the creative power of God's love. For all that I have done, I will pay. For all that I have left undone, I will pay. When the final card is turned, we will find that we cannot pay. The cost is beyond us; we cannot make it.

The Christian strives in a different direction. We do not strive for mastery over our souls. We strive to allow God to exercise that mastery. We become slaves of Jesus in order that we might become free. We lean not on our own efforts, but on the gift that God has given us in Jesus Christ. In Him we find the true reincarnation of God in our flesh. In Him we find the embodiment of our spirit in a spiritual body fit for the Kingdom of God. In Him we find deliverance from the mythology of men to walk in the revelation of God's love.

Symptoms and Solutions

As WE BEGIN TO DEAL with our transformation from the old Adam to the new man, we need to accentuate the positive, eliminate the negative, latch on to the affirmative and don't mess with ''Mister In-between.'' We need to realize that it is not in getting rid of all of the bad in us that makes us whole; it is growing up into something new in the power of the Holy Spirit. We must now enter into the resurrection life that awaits as we begin to say yes to God.

We are to release the old man within us to die. It is in that way that we find release from the sins that bind us. We are free to come out from behind the barriers of guilt that hide us. We hide to escape the death that is our just reward; and we miss the life that God is trying to give us in His presence. If we are to be delivered, we must be forgiven. We must confess our sin that God might have access to it. We must lay it out in the light of His love in order that He might remove it much as a doctor removes a cancer from the body.

Confession of sins to God in the presence of a minister has been rejected by many in the protestant churches because it has been required by the Roman Catholic church. The reformers were right; we have access to the throne of God. We may confess our sins to Him; but let's don't throw the baby out with the bath water. Confession is vital to our spiritual health; and we have been given the priviledge of confessing our sins to God in the presence of a witness who represents the whole church. We have been given the authority of Jesus to declare God's absolution and our own.

There is a therapeutic value of confession that has been set forth in the experience of those who are involved with spiritual healing; and affirmed by those who have found freedom through Alcoholics Anonymous. Confession unlocks the channel of God's grace to allow God to get to the inner wounds that need healing. It opens to the great physician both the symptoms—the deeds—and the sources—the motivations. It is the treatment of moral, emotional, and sometimes physical illness.

The use of confession in healing the sick is one of the suggestions of James. "Therefore confess your sins one to another, and pray for one another, that you may be healed. The prayer of a righteous man has great power in its effects." Ja 5:16 It helps both the one who is seeking to receive the power of God to heal, and the one who is seeking to offer himself as a channel for the healing power of God to flow.

When we are cluttered and fragmented with guilt and anxiety, we are not opened to being used effectively as channels. David du Plessis talks to us about "having ought against any." We need to forgive. Louise Eggleston admonished those whom she taught to clear the guilt by settling up with God. We need to confess and receive forgiveness. When we have both given and received forgiveness, we are better prepared to serve God as the Body of Christ.

Those who struggle with the power of alcohol in their lives know the great importance of confession in their lives. Those who "get the program" begin with the confession of their own problem. Step one must come before their deliverance. "We admitted that we were powerless over alcohol." Many have failed to find deliverance through AA because they would not take the first step.

Steps two and three are the beginning of the deliverance. We believe that there is a higher power, and we determined to turn the problem over to God as we understand him. That is the first step for any deliverance. Confession of the fault, and turning it over to God. For most of us it is easy to turn the impossible things over to God. We don't have anything to lose since we know that we cannot do it ourselves.

The fourth step is a continuation of the first. We made a fearless moral inventory. We looked for those things in our life that would help the enemy and hinder us. We searched out the self deceit, the resentment, the anxiety, and the rest of the negative elements of our life, and we confessed them to God AND TO ONE OTHER HUMAN BEING. Where possible, we made amends. The process is one that seeks to get at the root of the problem; and as we continue to seek, we continue to grow.

As most of us look at our lives, we feel that there are some things that we cannot handle. Those we are willing to turn over to the Lord. There are many other parts of life that we believe we can handle. Those are the source of most of our guilt. We do not reach our own expectations, and we feel guilty. We believe we should have done it better, and we feel guilty. These errors in our lives lie in the area that we need to turn over to the Lord daily as we continue to learn to walk with Him. We can do nothing good without Him, and so we stay grafted to the vine.

Some schools of psychology try to deal with sin by explaining it away. There is the feeling that we might shift the blame for things to someone else, and then we will be free. The young people of our generation have been taught to hold their parents responsible for their shortcomings. That takes away their own responsibility; but it leaves them in a position of despair. There is no way for them to deal with their problems. They have confessed the sins of their parents and not their own. They have cast their sins upon their parents, and there is no way for them to deal with them since they are out of their hands. Their need is to confess their own, and seek forgiveness of God and His grace and power to amend their lives. That is the only beginning that will bring them to freedom.

Even as the churches begin to follow the psychological leadership of the world, moving away from traditional forms of confession, the evidence shows that those who use confession enjoy better mental health. I have had a number of psychiatrists tell me that if people would use confession, it would remove a great portion of their work load. The conscience of man cannot be reasoned to a state of righteousness. It is cleansed through confession and the absolution of those sins confessed. The freedom does not lie in understanding our sins, but in the authority that Jesus has given to the Church, ''Whose soever sins ye remit, they are remitted unto them; and whose soever sins ye retain, they are retained.'' Jn 20:23

The fear of rejection by others weighs heavily on our decision to confess our sins. It is normally heavier than the burden of the sins that we carry. We are hesitant to reveal our hidden faults to anyone else. I have had more than a few people who come to confession for the first time, return after a time with some sin that they did not confess in their first confession. As we talk, it seems that they could trust me to hear all of the others without condemning them, but the one or two they dared not risk. As the Lord continues to work in their lives, and they find that I have not condemned them, they return with the rest of the burden.

There are many people who would rather face hell with their sins than let other people know that they have them. They covet the approval of their brethren so much that they hide. They feel that the brethren will never know—even if they go to hell. This is particularly true in fellowships where judgment and criticism are based on behavior codes. It is less prevalent in communities where love and acceptance is the basis for relationships.

We are much like the people who go into the doctor's office with our arm wrapped up because we have a bad cut. We have wrapped it in a towel to keep from bleeding, and likely because we cannot stand to look at it ourselves.

When the doctor comes in, he might say, ''Unwrap your arm and show me the cut.''

Our response might be, "I don't want to do that. It's too ugly. Besides it might bleed."

"If you don't unwrap it and show it to me, I can't do anything about it. I have to have access to it before I can treat it."

"But it's bleeding, and I don't want to look either. Why can't you do something for me without my showing it to you?"

The conversation is ridiculous; but it is much like our conversations with God about our sins. If we are to seek healing, we must give God access to all of the illness. We must confess all of the symptoms.

There have been books written on the subject of preparing for confession. I do not propose to write another. My suggestion to people who are preparing for a confession is (1) find a place where you can be quiet, and be still with God; (2) ask Jesus to bring the light of His forgiving love into your memory; (3) ask Holy Spirit to bring to remembrance those things that you need to confess; (4) with paper and pencil in hand, let your mind go back over each period of time in your life; and write down those things that seem to come to the mind with a feeling of needing confession. Let the Holy Spirit make the things clear to you. It is the Spirit who searches the depths of man's heart.

When your list is complete, you will likely have things on it that don't seem that important; and there may be other things that you think of later that should be on it. Use the list that the Spirit gives you. He may add other things to a list for a second confession. Trust the Spirit to lead you; and confess what He has given you now. The list will contain things for which you feel a resultant guilt. You felt guilt for them after you had done them. At the time you did them, you may have reasoned that it was all right, but the guilt is still there.

When I was young, I stole something from a department store. I did not feel guilty while I was doing it. The store had plenty. I knew that they wouldn't miss the merchandise. I rationalized it all. I felt a little fear of getting caught, but I felt no guilt. Later in thinking about what I had done, I felt guilty. The guilt was the result of the action. It stayed with me until I confessed it to God years later before an old priest who administered the absolution of God to me. At that point I could lay it to rest.

It is important in choosing a confessor—someone who can witness your confession to God—that you find someone who will forgive you rather than condemning you. If your witness condemns you, the guilt is reinforced. The authority that the Church has been given is to set men free or leave them bound. I believe that Jesus meant for us to set them free—not bind them. "There is now no condemnation for those who are in Christ Jesus." Rm 8:1 Seek someone who is willing to wield the authority to forgive.

If you are stuck in trying to find someone to hear your confession, find a priest. I have heard confessions for everyone from Pentecostals to Roman Catholics. There is a real advantage in using a priest or minister. They have generally heard enough so that they will not be shocked by what you say. They are also willing to pronounce God's absolution. Most of them can help you through the confession—to clarify and to put into right words the sins that you bring. (As an added asset, they cannot be brought into court to testify against you as some laymen might.)

There are many who want to confess their sins to God alone. Some may be able to do this; I cannot. Most people who argue against using the traditional order for confession will say, ''I confess my sins to myself.'' The words themselves speak the truth of what so often happens. I think about the sin; I am sorry that I did it, and I tuck it away inside myself.

The use of a confessor keeps me from wallowing in my sin. He keeps me from explaining my sins to God or rationalizing my actions. He continually brings me back from explanation to confession. God already understands. He does not look for me to explain my sin or repress my sin. He wants me to confess my sin—to open it to Him to treat with His love. The confessor helps me to maintain that posture before God.

When I hear myself and know that someone else has also heard all of my sins, I cannot tuck them back inside. I can only release them to the Lord. When I hear His forgiveness proclaimed, I know that I am set free. Some inner release occurs that can occur in no other way that I have found. It is tragic when people confuse counselling with confession and miss the power of release that we have in Jesus Christ.

One of the great disappointments that we encounter in using confession is that we repent of some of our sins, but not all. We feel that if we repeat some of the sins, we have failed to live up to our end of the bargain. We often feel that if we were truly repentant, we would not sin again. When we do, we feel that our confession was insincere. I used to be very critical of my Roman Catholic brethren who would go to confession one day and sin the next. My judgment was that they didn't care. The truth was that I didn't want to go to confession because I was afraid that I would do the same thing.

When I first made my confession, I did it because I was being ordained. I knew that I would be hearing confessions, and I thought I had better try it out first. I found that some of the sins that I confessed repeated; but there were others which were removed from my life completely. As I continued to use the discipline, I discovered that other sins fell away also.

It seems to me to follow the treatment of physical needs. I have been to the doctor with some things that required nothing but a shot, and they were treated. There are other ailments that need greater care. I once had surgery that required that I return to the doctor for treatment a number of times before healing was complete. Those who have a disease such as leprosy, will be treated for the rest of their lives; but treatment is still desirable for dealing with any disease—those that are quickly healed as well as those that take great time.

It is in the continued penitence and confession that the healing light of Jesus is allowed to shine on both my short term and my chronic illness of the spirit. My healing comes as He is able to change me at the very core of my being. I am delivered from guilt at each one of my visits to the confessional. I am delivered from Sin as the creative power of God's love works within me.

INNER HEALING

There is in each of us a bank of memory tapes that have a record of every moment of our life. The little electrical circuits in our brain hold not only the sight and sound, but also the feelings that we were experiencing at the time. As these little circuits assemble in the mind, they form complexes of memories that help us deal with the world we live in. When we have been close enough to the fire to know heat, we begin to form a complex that enables us to know that when we see a fire, we better watch out or we might be burned. If we have been burned, we might feel undue fear of fire. Without these complexes, we could not be able to function in a new situation or an old one. Everything would be a new adventure to us.

Any trauma in my life is apt to be felt repeatedly as I pass through similar situations. As I see people that may have been a part of my trauma, I will have the feeling return. As I enter the same sort of material situation, the feeling might surface again. As I seek to use my past experience to deal with my present circumstance, the feeling will come to the surface at that conscious level along with the sight and sound memory. I will feel something in my reaction that has nothing to do with the present.

A young wife who was having trouble relating to her husband sexually came for counsel. She had an aversion to sex that involved acute anxiety and fear. She loved her husband, and wanted to relate to him, but she was not able to curb the feelings. As we discussed the past, it came to light that she had been molested by one of her family when she was young. There had been a great deal of stir about it, and the parental anxiety was magnified by her fear and anxiety within the experience. It was that feeling that assaulted her when she was with her husband.

After she became aware of the problem, she could seek to build a better relationship to her husband; but the feeling was still there. We needed to go back to the little girl in whose life the trauma was recorded, and allow the love of Jesus to set her free. We know that we cannot go back and relive any part of our lives. Whatever happened yesterday is gone.

Jesus, however, is not limited by time and space. He is able to go back into each situation of our life and heal it. He does not change what happened—that would be to alter history. He can and does change our perception of what happened; and with that He can change the feeling content of our memories. In the case of the young wife, we asked that He go back and heal the trauma that she felt—to show His love to the little one who felt guilty and dirty and unacceptable. We asked that He bring His love and peace to the little one who was bound in fear that she might be set free. We used our holy imagination to see Him holding the little girl and comforting her. We asked Him to heal the relationship with her busband—to remove the fear and anxiety and replace it with love and joy.

There was a dramatic change in the woman's relationship to her husband. It was not all perfect; but she was able to enter into a positive growth pattern that had been blocked by the emotional memories that she had brought to her marriage. The positive experience continues to grow and be reinforced. The old memory has been cleansed of its emotional content; the new set of feelings is beginning to take shape.

It is not always necessary for us to visualize the past experience in order to be healed; but it seems helpful in reinforcing the healing. In my own life there was a healing of acute anxiety and insecurity that I had in my childhood. When the prayer for healing was offered, the picture of the little boy came to my mind. He was sobbing his heart out in the presence of two adults who were arguing. Jesus walked over to the little one and put His hand on his head; and the peace and joy of God were given to the little one. I have felt the freedom in the present. The imagination of the healing process has been a great source of comfort to me as I find new evidence of the healing in my life.

When I pray for someone else, I find it helpful to ask the one for whom I am praying to try to see the little one for whom we pray. Most of the time they are able to remember the one that needs the healing, and then tell me how the little one feels. We then invite Jesus to come and bring healing and forgiveness to the little one. If there is need for the child to forgive, the forgiveness is articulated. We then ask Jesus to come and enable that forgiveness to be given. When the person is able to see Jesus with the little one of the past, we then ask how the little one is feeling now. Some of the healing seems to be slow, but there is usually an immediate change in what the person sees in his past.

Since the emotional content that is being healed has likely been reinforced through the life of the person, the healing might very well be progressive. In my own experience, one of the areas of my life that was healed in the present was my ability to speak on the floor of a Church convention. In the past,

I got sick at nearly every convention, and I was unable to speak without a gripping fear. Since that time, I have become increasingly free.

Jesus redeems the time. That time which we live without an awareness of His presence is lived in hell. That may be painful or pleasant depending on circumstances. It is redeemed by inviting Him in. Whether it is the past, present, or future; where Jesus is received, redemption is manifest. He comes into the old to make it a new creation.

The presence of Jesus is not imaginary; it is real. It is not something that is added to the past. He was there all of the time. He was simply not seen or felt. I remember clearly the little boy in my past saying, "Jesus, where were you? I couldn't see you," as Jesus came to him. The truth was that I did not know Him then. The prayer request is simply for Jesus to show us the reality of that particular time in His presence rather than what we perceived as truth and recorded in our heart. It is redeeming the time.

The broken heart is mended when Jesus comes into the break. With His love He creates a new record of life that we have in our experience. We are no longer bound to react as we have reacted in the past. We are being set free to respond to God in the new situations of our life. Jesus answers the prayer of the psalmist, "Create in me a new heart, O God, and renew a right spirit in me." Ps 51:10

In seeking someone to intercede for us as we seek the healing of our broken hearts, we need to choose someone who is loving. We also need someone who is willing to experiment with God—someone who trusts that God's promises are true and that He is able to overcome all things. We need someone who is willing to walk with us from hell into heaven. We need one who will listen without condemnation; and whose imagination will help us open our past to Jesus. We seek one who is patient and willing to wait on the Lord.

With the simplicity of the task, it is a wonder that there is not an abundance of Christians who are willing to offer themselves for this ministry. The truth is that to date such people are few and far between. Some are reluctant to try something new; but the risk is quite small when we consider that it is no more than our inviting Jesus into our own lives and into the lives of others in specific ways.

Such prayer delivers us from bondage to the past to set us free to choose without undue pull from our memories. We are delivered into the freedom that Jesus brings to our lives when He comes. We are free to know and to experience the Kingdom of God in a new dimension.

Inner healing is not the same thing as confession. When we spoke of guilt as being resultant guilt in confession, we might speak of attendant guilt being dealt with in inner healing. We accumulate attendant guilt when we feel guilty as we are passing through some experience. It is recorded even while we are committing the sinful act. Often guilt that we pick up in this way is not relieved by confession; but it can be relieved by inner healing.

EXORCISM

There are those who are living with compulsive patterns of life or those who are pulled in two directions when making decisions. These people may sometimes be released through the use of exorcism. The general symptoms that might be dealt with through the use of exorcism are any actions that seem to be against my own will. These actions will either be as a result of our reaction patterns that we wrote of in inner healing, or the indwelling of some spirit that would take us in a different direction with our life.

Another symptom might be recognized as fragmentation of our will so that we don't even know what we want. This may range from mild ambivalence to acute schizophrenia. That is not to say that all ambivalence or schizophrenia is caused by some level of possession; it is to say that some can be relieved through the use of exorcism. That would lead us to think that some emotional illness is caused by possession.

Spirital bondage occurs in a number of different ways. I can be bound by my reactions to my mother or father when I was young. The bondage might be resentment or pride or rejection or any number of other symptoms of love gone amiss. It is as I rebel against my parents that I am imprinted by their virtues and their sins. It is only as I forgive them and forgive myself that I can be set free.

In praying to set people free from such bondage, we simply ask Jesus to cut through the bonds that we have used to deal with our relationships because we did not know love. We ask Him to cut through the fear, terror, and dread; through the anxiety and tensions; through the self-hate, self-condemnation, and self-punishment to set us free from the others and to set others free from us. We must be set free so that we might let love grow to transform all of our relationships that all might be set free.

We seek to be delivered from bondage to human emotions so we can come closer to the freedom that we can find in love alone. Love never binds either the lover or the object when we are in God's will. It is not possessive neither is it possessed. It is what we see when we look to Jesus as our example. It is achieved as we release the control of the world in which we live to God in the sure knowledge that He will bring His order into our lives.

In dealing with the problem of emotional bondage, the results are not always as fast as we might like; but at times they are quite dramatic. A young wife came into the office one day with a pressing problem. She and her husband were going to visit his family. The wife had a very strong resentment against the mother-in-law. She had been criticized early in the early stages of the marriage, and she had built up a bondage relationship. She was not able to forgive her mother-in-law.

We prayed simply that she might be set free from bondage to her mother-in-law in every way in order that she might be able to love her. The process was simple—we layed our hands on her and asked Jesus to come with the sword of His spirit to cut through the bonds of resentment so that she could love her mother-in-law with Jesus' love. The visit was not near the disaster that she had thought it would be. She had grown to actually love her old enemy.

There are also within some people the minions of Satan. It might be Satan himself or one of his lieutenants. This is not to be a matter of concern. Satan does have access to the old man within us. If we find him within, he is on his own ground. The other demons are those he brings with him as he comes to possess his territory within us. I have come to practice casting out Satan at each exorcism right after I pray for the cutting of bonds to the people and things of the world.

The issue has already been settled. We are purchased with a price; and as we claim our freedom in the Name of Jesus, Satan can no longer bind us. He must turn us loose. When this is followed by an invitation to Jesus to occupy that part of us that has been set free, we move from the old creation to the new. That part of us which is transferred from one kingdom to another is safe from being repossessed. That part of us which is not given into the protective care of Jesus is still open to being occupied again by Satan.

I spent a good bit of time trying to cast out a spirit from a young man who was to be baptized the following day. As yet he had not come to the waters of baptism to publicly affirm his new life in Christ Jesus—the adoption ceremony had not yet occurred. My wife had done some discernment for us, and we determined that there was a spirit named Achariba that plagued the young man. As the exorcism began, the spirit began to shout his name together with a number of other choice bits of nonsense.

I worked with the young man for about an hour before it became evident that I was not making any progress. There was no question about the spirit's presence. I had no question about the authority of Jesus to set him free; and so I went back to Jesus to seek His wisdom in the matter. I asked, "Lord, what do we do now?"

He answered, "You can stay here and play with the spirit all night if you wish; but it will not leave until Robert is baptized. He will leave then without any further resistance." This confirmed something that I read from Cyprian, an early Bishop of the Church in Africa, "Though the demons may persist up until the waters of baptism, they will not prevail beyond that."

The next day when the baptism was administered, the spirit was cast out and has given the young man no trouble since. It was a case of setting the new ground that the spirit could not walk in him. There was no shouting or yelling involved in the matter on the part of the exorcist; the demon was a little unruly, but not unduly.

There is no great formula or incantation that we must use to exercise the authority of Jesus. We simply command the spirit in the Name of Jesus to leave. We do not have to shout. Demons are not deaf. We do have to know whose authority we bear; and we have to be willing to commit God to the action He has directed us to do in His name.

There are times when the works of the flesh might be relieved through exorcism. I have seen many people who were bound by acute anxiety set free to walk in the peace of God by casting out a spirit of anxiety. I have seen one woman healed of rheumatoid arthritis through the exorcism of a spirit of resentment. These would seem to be the motivational forces that dwell within us as carnal men. These spirits seem to be the furnishings of our inner life that we are to trade in for the fruit of the Spirit.

My first encounter with exorcism myself grew out of an outburst of anger against my oldest son. I knew that it was against my will, and I knew that I was not in control of the situation. I determined to go share my experience of exorcism with a friend; and when I had finished, I asked him if he would be willing to pray for my deliverance from anger. He did; and since that time I have not had the same problem with the anger.

The purpose of exorcising such spirits is only to set us free to receive the fruit of the Spirit within. It is a matter of cultivating the garden of God. It is pulling weeds in order that the fruit might grow. We may simply cast them out in the Name of Jesus as we did with Satan and his friends.

I have heard many different techniques used in the practice of exorcism. I have been led to place my hand on the head of the person and ask for protection, and the power to be an instrument of God. "Lord Jesus, we thank you for being with us in power. We ask that you pour out your Spirit upon us that we may be of one accord—that we may become an instrument of your peace. I claim the power and protection of the Blessed Trinity for all of those present and all of those near from every spirit contrary to the Holy Spirit; and I call upon the power of the Name of the Lord Jesus, and the power of His most precious blood that this person might be set free from all bondage."

I then place my hand on the small of the person's back and command the spirit to depart. "Satan, I bind you in the Name of Jesus and by the power of His blood I command you to go to Jesus to find your appointed place. Spirit of fear, I command you to come out in the Name of Jesus. I command you to go to Jesus to be consumed in the fire of His love.'' I am sure that the Spirit might lead others to use different ways of doing the work. My suggestion to everyone is to ask the Lord to lead, and follow as you are led.

At the close of an exorcism, I ask Jesus to fill the person with the Holy Spirit, and bring forth within him the fruit of the Spirit so that there might be no room for any spirit to return. As the fruit of the Spirit take root and grow within the person, they not only fill the voids, but they begin to choke out the other weeds that infest the garden of God. We are delivered from bondage to the spirits into the freedom of the Holy Spirit through the process of exorcism.

Ghosts, Gates and Gospel

OUR DISCUSSION OF SPIRITS of the departed who might still make themselves known on earth is found in chapter nine on spiritualism. It is likely the most controversial of the problems to be faced in deliverance. Since it is impossible for us to verify reality beyond death, we cannot submit conclusive evidence that what we say is true. We can consider the data that our experiences have yielded, and draw some conclusions about the matter.

Symptoms of being indwelt by a spirit of another person who has departed the body are ambivalence or feeling like we want to do two things at the same time. Some people have an even clearer manifestation in the emergence of a completely different personality in some instances. *The Three Faces of Eve* sets forth a case of a multiple personality that includes three possible different persons in one body.

The early fathers felt that many of those who were possessed were buffeted by spirits of the departed who had not been laid to rest. The first Christian martyr, Justin, was one of these. One of the English exorcists, Christopher Niell-Smith, told me one time that there are people in the English Church who believe that all possession is by the departed, although he believed that there is a variety of spirits in the unseen realm.

If the spirit with which we deal is a departed soul rather than a demon, then we must deal with him as such. The gospel is first preached. The soul must be told that it is loved by Jesus who has died in order that all might be reconciled to the Father. That might seem strange, but it is in accord with I Peter. We are certainly not to cast anyone into hell—even if we could. We are not to deal with them in any way different from the way we would deal with one in the flesh.

We do not approach the spirit as if the spirit has information that we need, but as if we have the information that the spirit needs. Where there seems to be a positive response to the gospel, we might absolve the spirit. That is the authority that we have been given by Jesus. That is the authority we are called to wield in the life of every man who will receive it with penitence.

I used to be concerned that some of the spirits were not truly penitent. After all they were found in a place that they did not belong. It dawned on me that I pronounce absolution every Sunday to many who are penitent, and to some who are not. God is the One who forgives, we just pronounce. If the spirit is not penitent, I have done nothing. If the spirit is penitent, then I have set one of God's people free to come to Him.

When I first encountered such a spirit, I was led to baptize it. In the process it occurred to me that this would be the only reason for the baptism for the dead to which Paul refers. I have subsequently been led to ask Jesus to baptize them in the river of living water that flows from the throne of God. I cannot see the river, but I believe that it is there, and I have seen something happen that enabled people to be set free through that ministry.

The next step is to introduce them to Jesus. They can see Him but they do not know Him. It was from George Bennett's tract on his experience with such a spirit that I have begun to send them to the Shining One. They seem to be able to see Him when their attention is called to that quality of light that Jesus has in the Kingdom. There have been some who have been afraid that the light would burn them. That assurance I have also learned to make. It will not burn.

I ask Jesus to come and take their hand and lead them to the place that is prepared for them in the Kingdom. He comes, but He seems to wait for each one to reach out. He waits until they want to go with Him. That is the decision that is preached. There is no reason to fear. In Jesus there is no condemnation and there is no punishment. Somehow, they seem to know that what is preached is true. It takes a while for some to move; others move easily and quickly to meet Jesus and go with Him into life.

There are also those who seem to want to live their own life without Jesus. They also want a body in which to live it; and so they take one that belongs to someone else. These do not move so easily. They must be cast out with the help of the angels who can do that which we cannot do ourselves.

One of the first cases that I met and dealt with that was a difficult matter was of John. He came walking into my church one day with a blank stare. He was the director of the local children's theater and he had just gone through a night in which he had torn up all of the sets and costumes that he had made. He stopped, and stared for a moment and asked, "Can you help me?"

I replied, "I don't know, but we'll sure try to see what we can do about it. Are you willing to try exorcism?"

"I'll try anything," he mumbled.

I called the person that I used for discernment and received the information that there was a spirit named Bill. I called one of my ministers who happened to be a friend of John's to pray with me, and we went to the altar to seek deliverance for John and for Bill. We preached to Bill, we absolved him, and we were urging him to go with Jesus, when John suddenly asked, "Why can't I go and let him stay here?" It was a good question, but I have always thought that God put us in the right body for us. We don't have a choice in the matter of trading.

After a time, the spirit left, and John showed a drastic change as peace came to him for the first time since we had started praying. He left the church and went immediately down to the Cathedral to ask one of the priests to say a votive Mass to St. John, Baptist. I did not see him for six months. He attributed his healing to the Mass at first. He could accept that. As he grew toward a measure of integrity within himself, he was able to see what had happened.

John pursued a vocation as a monk. He tried all of the known orders to see if he fit in any of the disciplines. He finally made up his own rule of life, took his vows before the Bishop of the Diocese, and entered the religious life. He was set free from the bondage that led him to destroy his work periodically. He has a stable grip on life, and continues to grow in the Lord. He has a vital and creative ministry to children.

I do not know what happened to Bill. We felt assured that he had made his contact with Jesus and that he had made his peace with Jesus. There is no reason for me to believe that he is anywhere other than in the Kingdom with Jesus. I know that it is God's will that we all enter the Kingdom. I believe that when we say yes, He brings it to pass. It is hard for me to believe that He changes His mind about us when we die.

The freedom that John found was not simply freedom for John. It was also freedom for Bill. It made possible the reconciliation for which Jesus died. I would presume that he now prays for John among the communion of saints rather than leading him to destroy the work that God had put to his hand.

There have been enough of these incidents for me to believe that they are what they appear to be. There may be some other way to explain the experiences; but I don't think that there is an easier explanation, nor is there one any more in accord with the scriptures. It is more a matter of being opposed to our images that we normally use in dealing with the reality of death and the life that follows.

I have seen enough people set free through this ministry that I still use it. For ten years I have been seeking objections to it from history and from scripture, and I have found none. There is an inordinate fear by some that we are dealing with spiritualism or reincarnation. We are not dealing with spiritualism because we are not seeking to hear from the dead but to preach to them. We are not dealing with reincarnation in the common meaning of the term because we do not believe that the spirits are in a new body that is their own. The truth is that they are misplaced; and in their misplacement they furnish the believers in reincarnation with most of their data.

It would seem that there are some people walking around as inadvertant mediums. They carry with them spirits that do not belong within them. We may deal with them as demons if we choose; but if we are to obey the admonition of Jesus, we will preach the gospel to them, absolve them, and seek to bring them to Jesus even as we do in the flesh.

There are many who do not want it to be possible for us to be reconciled to God after death. There was a time when I felt the same. I believed that they ought to get what they deserved. I did well with that until I began to meditate on what would happen if I got what I deserved. If there were a vote in the Kingdom, I would vote with God. I would like to see them all there.

I would close this chapter with a story of a vision that was shared by Bernie Warfield, a Baptist from Detroit. Bernie saw himself with all of the rest of the people in the Kingdom sitting at the great banquet table. All was ready for the feast except that Jesus' chair was empty. As they waited, Bernie decided to go and look for Him.

He found Him finally gazing out of a window, and he said, "Lord, come on. Everything is ready, and the people are waiting." The Lord turned and looked at Bernie and said, "You go on. I am waiting for Judas."

Delivered Into Life

Wʜᴇɴ SOMETHING IS CAST out of a person, there must be something put it. The Church of the first century used exorcism as a preparation for baptism. The vestiges of that action are still used in some of the modern rituals. I heard Aleander Schmeeman of St. Vladimir's seminary speak once about baptism.

He began with the statement that we must take something out before we put something new in. We cast out the bad spirits from a baby before we ask God to put the good Spirit in. It is based on the understanding that we need to be changed from the spirit out. We cannot make the Kingdom simply by changing our actions.

When we cast out Satan, we ask God to fill the person with the Holy Spirit that the new ground might be claimed in the Kingdom. We are not able to hold the ground that is gained in our own strength. We seek one who is able to keep us free.

When we cast out the spirits that seem to be the works of the flesh such as anger, resentment, fear, etc.; we ask God to fill us with the fruit of the Spirit. It is in the fruit that we receive that which displaces the negative spirits that are cast out. It is love that displaces fear. It is peace that displaces anxiety. It is the divinity of Jesus that displaces the humanity that is ours.

It is only as we pursue our deliverance to this goal that we can truly say that we are delivered. It is only as we pursue our healing to this goal that we can say that we are completely healed. As a general rule we are somewhere on the road to our predestination in the Kingdom of God. It is as we pursue that road to its end that we find our salvation. God is easy to please but He is hard to satisfy. He continues to call us to the perfection that He has already prepared for us in Christ Jesus.

It is not an easy matter to talk to the spirits that you cannot see, and expect them to obey. I have found myself in the midst of an exorcism wondering what in the world I am doing talking at a person's back at a spirit that might or might not be there. I have found that their experience of freedom as they change the spirit within for the Holy Spirit is enough to keep me going even though I feel like a fool at times.

When we seek to walk with Jesus, we need to receive the Holy Spirit. It is not optional for us to seek Him; it is mandatory. It is not necessary for us to have an experience that is identical to someone else's. It is essential for us to have one that is for us—tailor made to fit our particular life. It is in the Spirit that we find the life of Jesus in us.

It is easy for us to seek to walk ahead of Jesus. We have gotten a glimpse of the Kingdom and we have gone ahead of the King to bring it in. One of the great problems that others have with new Christians is that they are out to save the world overnight. When they find that the power of God is real, they want to wield it to bring all men into the Kingdom of God.

Those who run ahead of Jesus are apt to find the going tough. He has told us, "Take my yoke upon you and learn of me, for my yoke is easy and my burden is light." Mt. 11:29 When we are yoked with Jesus and we try to get ahead of Him, we find that we are trying to pull the whole load. If we continue to try it, we are in some danger of despairing.

When we tend to sit down and drag behind Jesus, we will find that we are dragged along in the pain of not being in step with the Lord. We are constantly having to deal with things that we would rather put off. Our growth loses all of its joy. We walk almost as if our neck is caught in the yoke and we are being pulled by the one who is moving the load.

It is when we are at one with Jesus that we can move by His side, and we find that He is the one who pulls the weight. We walk with Him while He carries even us. This is the goal we seek as we ask to be filled with the Spirit. We seek to become the reincarnation of Jesus of Nazareth—risen from the dead, and present to bring us into the wholeness of the Kingdom of Our God.